# THE JOY OF ENGLISH

# THE
# JOY OF
# ENGLISH

## JESSE KARJALAINEN

**100 illuminating conversations about the English language**

**howto**books

First published in Great Britain in 2012 by
How To Books Ltd
Spring Hill House
Spring Hill Road
Begbroke, Oxford
OX5 1RX, United Kingdom

info@howtobooks.co.uk
www.howtobooks.co.uk

First Edition published 2012

British Library Cataloguing in Publication Data.
A catalogue record for this book is available from the British Library.

ISBN 978 1 84528 478 7

Produced for How To Books by Deer Park Productions, Tavistock
Cover design by Jesse Karjalainen/Frédérique Swist
'The Joy of English' logo design by Jesse Karjalainen
Printed and bound in Great Britain by the MPG Books Group

# CONTENTS

# CONTENTS BY SUBJECT

# PREFACE

There are hundreds of books about English, so why write another one? In many ways, *The Joy of English* is aimed at a popular audience and intended as an antidote to books that either put people off or put them to sleep.

I believe that a common difficulty for people wanting to improve their English skills has been to think, "Ah, I must go out and buy myself a book about grammar." So they go out and do exactly that. However, pretty soon they become bogged down in a coma-inducing tome about transitive verbs, gerunds and unattached participles. Their enthusiasm quickly evaporates and they never open the book again.

What they want is help with their English, but what they get instead is a depressing feeling that English was never their subject to begin with.

In response, my aim was to write a book that gives good advice about the English language without getting caught up in moral panics or the minutiae of grammar and parts of speech. I have written a book that gets straight to the point and provides the answers to common questions without – I hope – putting anyone off.

Instead of being a complete book of grammar or punctuation, or an exhaustive A–Z of language terms, *The Joy of English* is about only those areas that I feel will improve and elevate your language skills the fastest. The 100 chapters presented in this book essentially comprise the 100 most common grey areas that cause the most day-to-day confusion and doubt.

Some people will take the inevitable position that language is always changing and therefore, "it does not matter". To them I would say: the advice included in this book is presented in the form of tools rather than rules. Ignore them at your pleasure. But remember, even if you don't care about language and how you use it, there are many other people who do. And they might be the ones reading your next memo/e-mail/letter, etc. If it is important to them then it should be important to you.

*The Joy of English* arose from my genuine passion and interest in the everyday workings of the English language. My goal is to make learning about English usage interesting and, above all, useful in your own communication, whether for work, home or study. There are inevitably going to be those who disagree with certain points that I make in this book, especially if the truth goes against what they previously knew to be true. But I hope that they recognise the broader contribution that I am trying to make when it comes to showing the way towards better English for all who ever wondered but were too afraid to ask.

One frequently heard phrase in such debates is, "but you know what I mean, so it does not really matter". In many cases, we do know what you mean. But what is often overlooked is that, not only do we know what you mean, we also know what you do not mean. You can walk round all day with spinach in your teeth and not by bothered by it, but rarely does anyone leave it there once alerted to its presence.

If we are honest, most of us do care about language and how it is used – when we know how. Others say that attempts to "regulate" language never work. I say, what about dictionaries, spell checkers and education? Do these not regulate successfully? If it really "did not matter", then we would never use or own dictionaries. We would just make up our own meanings to words and expect others to catch on. When it comes to usage the answers aren't always as easy as, for example, looking up a particular spelling. So we ask around and hope for the best. If we make a mistake, we won't know anyway. The problem is that no one has ever pointed things out to us – at least not in a constructive, considerate way.

One of the big fears that a lot of people have is that good grammar, perhaps like fine wine, is a world that they know nothing about. This makes it seem scary or intimidating to even entertain the thought of taking an interest in the subject. Second, and unfortunately because of the way that certain "educated" people may behave towards those who are not "in the know", a lot of people perceive both grammar and wine to be only for snobs. Despite secretly having a genuine interest in it, many will shy away from it because of a lack of confidence in their abilities.

The good news is that you don't need a degree in winemaking to learn about and take an interest in wine. And you do not need a degree in linguistics to learn about and take an interest in English.

But what about grammar?

Grammar is, for all intents and purposes, a red herring. If you speak English, then you already know its grammar. All you need now is to be shown a few rights and wrongs. Sure, you can also learn more about grammar for its own sake, just as you could learn about the detailed processes of how wine is made. However, such things are not for everyone. The same is true with grammar. There is no shame in that.

Turning the tables, *The Joy of English* is written to be more palatable than books that focus squarely on grammar (there are enough of those). Instead of teaching you about such terms as conjugation, nominative and preterite, each chapter is dedicated to a common error, myth, problem or bad habit that many of us are prone to use without knowing it.

Everyone has the ability to be better at English. All it takes is a point in the right direction, a couple of good examples as a model and a reasonable amount of practise. This book's 100 chapters represent some of the most frequently asked questions about English. The bite-sized chapters are not complete guides to, say, how to use an apostrophe. Instead, they look specifically at those parts that usually goes wrong, such as getting "its" and "it's" wrong. They avoid going over things that you will most probably know as a speaker of English already. This saves you time and effort by concentrating on what you need to know.

There are many components of good English, of which grammar is just one. Other areas include spelling, punctuation and style. This book explores a range of these essential areas. Grammar, of course, does come into the picture. But not always. The first chapter, about why the word *very* is often not needed, does not involve grammar. The chapter on tautologies (Chapter 6) – why just impulse is better than sudden impulse – has nothing to do with grammar, despite what many people believe. And the differences between British and US spelling (Chapter 71), not to mention commonly misspelt words (Chapter 64), have nothing to do with grammar, yet they are important.

We all learn in different ways, so the book can be used in various ways. Readers can choose to browse, dipping in at will, or they can read from cover to cover. The book can be read through completely once just to get a handle on things and return to each specific chapter when the need calls. Alternatively, those who prefer can focus on the examples alone – there are 1500 to enjoy.

Each chapter is ordered so that the most important information is at the beginning. There will typically be several examples to begin with, then a condensed summary in bold giving you the outline, or a reminder when you look it up later. Then what follows is usually the nuts and bolts, followed by deeper discussion for those who are interested enough to know more about the reasons, history, etc. And that is all there is to it.

For those of you already feeling the urge to resist being told what to do, have no fear. There are more carrots in this book than sticks, and what you choose to do is up to you alone. Some chapters even provide several alternatives and leave the ball firmly in your court (Chapter 88), while others challenge the status quo and ask whether it is time for change (Chapter 34).

To use one, final analogy, language is a lot like fashion. Fashions come and go but style always remains cool. There are no rules, only tradition and convention. The way you speak to your friends and family does not matter. However, the way you speak at a job interview may well be more considered. How you speak to your co-workers will differ from how you communicate the day the Queen visits your place of work. It should not matter what we wear, but imagine turning up to your own wedding wearing a pair of jeans. You are right, there are no rules. But if it matters to important people around you, it should matter to you. Just try going to a job interview wearing only a dressing gown and see where that gets you. In the same way, writing privately is different from being a sign writer or news reporter, when your words go out in public.

Yes, language is always changing – but not of its own accord. Language is not a living entity, it is a system of communication between living beings. It changes because people change it. People change it because they know no better (mistakes) or because they want to change it (slang). Fashion, too, is always changing, but a lot of what changes comes and goes quickly. Few would dream or dare to sport a mullet, let alone insist that everyone else wear one too. Few people wear non-matching socks, yet there is no rule that says we shouldn't. The truth is that, when it comes to the English language, only a small percentage has actually changed in the last few centuries. Certain things come and go, but strip away the fads – whether words like gnarly or stonewash jeans – what remains are still the fundamentals. Nouns are still nouns, sentences are still sentences and the language is still English. A suit still functions as a suit whether it is made from the finest cloth or purple PVC, and socks are still worn inside shoes instead of on the outside.

This book is ideal for the home and the workplace, as well as for study. It is ideal as a refresher, even for the professional writer. *The Joy of English* will provide you with a deeper understanding of English usage and alert you to the pitfalls to avoid. Keep it on your desk at the ready, rather than gathering dust on your highest shelf. And most of all, enjoy it and have fun doing so. As you become comfortable and more familiar with the myriad areas of usage found in this book you are sure to begin seeing language in a new way – with greater confidence. I truly believe that this book will change your English for ever.

Jesse Karjalainen
Bristol

# THE
# JOY OF
# ENGLISH

# A SHORT GRAMMAR

If you are completely unfamiliar with grammar, here are five essential terms that you should know.

**noun**     = another word for "things", whether person or object, real or imaginary (e.g. book, plan, strategy, Paul, home, dream).

**verb**     = another word for "actions", or "doing" words. Verbs tell us how or what happens or happened (e.g. spoke, cheat, won, describe, exercised, write).

**adjective**     = a type of word or several words that describe or give more information about "things" (nouns). Adjectives do not describe verbs (e.g. deep, sharp, blue, heavy, large, overweight).

**adverb**     = a type of word or several words that describe "actions" (verbs), adjectives or other adverbs. Adverbs do not describe "things" (nouns) (e.g. deeply, sincerely, well, often, quickly, not).

**clause**     = in simple terms, think of a clause as being a small sentence inside a larger sentence, or one of several statements expressed within a single sentence (e.g. I am tired + because I went to bed late last night. We saw a film + and Dad bought us popcorn. I told you yesterday + that today is my birthday).

# 04

## who versus whom
### *Whom is not yet doomed*

✓ **I want to know who did what to whom.**
✗ *I want to know who did what to who.*
✓ **To whom it may concern.**
✗ *To who it may concern.*
✓ **For whom the bell tolls.**
✗ *For who the bell tolls.*
✓ **They always preach to whomever will listen.**
✗ *They always preach to whoever will listen.*

**If you remember anything at all about using *who* and *whom*, it must be this: *whom* rather than *who* is used directly after words such as *to*, *by*, *for*, *at*, *in*, *with*, *from*, *towards* and *of* etc. At a more in-depth level, use *whom* when *who* is the object.**

I have several pieces of advice when it comes to using *who/whom*. First, *who* will become *whom* almost without fail when it directly follows words (prepositions) like *about*, *at*, *by*, *in*, *for*, *from*, *of*, *towards*, *with* etc.:

✓ **about whom**        ✓ **at whom**
✓ **by whom**           ✓ **in whom**
✓ **for whom**          ✓ **from whom**
✓ **of whom**           ✓ **towards whom**
✓ **with whom**         ✓ **without whom**

✗ *about who*           ✗ *at who*
✗ *by who*              ✗ *in who*
✗ *for who*             ✗ *from who*
✗ *of who*              ✗ *towards who*
✗ *with who*            ✗ *without who*

This simple rule goes a long way towards getting *who/whom* right and serves as a great starting point – all without knowing a shred of grammar.

The second thing to remember is that when it comes to casual conversation, there is nothing wrong with simply using *who* every time. Shocking as this suggestion may sound, *who* is not likely to be misunderstood. You can use it safe in the knowledge that 90% of people will find it acceptable. Few will take offence because the word *whom* is in many respects on the endangered-species list in this regard. Many people – especially those born around the 1970s and later – get by perfectly well using *who* in place of *whom* without any problems or concerns.

For many, these first two approaches are enough to get by with. Nevertheless, the correct usage of *whom* is often treated as a shibboleth that marks a "good education" – so take care, especially in formal circles.

For those wanting a clearer explanation, the third piece of advice is to say that *who* must always be *whom* when expressed in the object form. This can seem an easy concept but it is a lot trickier to put into practice.

*Whom* is an example of an old form of English that has survived beyond its use-by date. Before you begin to write me an angry letter in protest, let me elaborate. Of the approximately 1 million words in the English language, *who* (as well as the derivatives *whoever* and *whomever*) is one of only six words that have different subject/object forms. The other five are: *I*, *he*, *they*, *she* and *we*.

| SUBJECT | OBJECT |
|---|---|
| I | *me* |
| he | *him* |
| they | *them* |
| she | *her* |
| we | *us* |
| who | *whom* |

From this perspective, the difference between *who* and *whom* is seemingly clear: *whom* is the object form of *who* and few will be confused about which of the following examples are correct:

| | |
|---|---|
| With I? | *With me?* |
| With she? | *With her?* |
| With he? | *With him?* |
| With we? | *With us?* |
| With they? | *With them?* |
| With who? | *With whom?* |

In this context the difference between the two seems simple enough. Herein lies the real reason that people have so much difficulty with *who/ whom*: it is that they have difficulty understanding the difference between subject and object.

> This is Jesse, who wrote that book. (*subject*)
> This is Jesse, whom you have been asking about. (*object*)

All of a sudden the *who/whom* game is no longer so much fun. Both of these examples use *who/whom* according to the same principles stated in the lists above, but I can guarantee you that a lot of people will find the difference far from obvious. Is the following example correct or incorrect according to subject/object principles?

> I have no idea whom she decided to confide in.

When put on the spot, not everyone will have the confidence to say that this sentence is, indeed, correct. (The clue is that *whom* refers to a third party, someone other than *she*.) The problem with *whom* is that this lack of confidence means that using it correctly has not only become cumbersome for many, but also that it no longer sounds natural in casual language. *Whom* runs the risk of sounding stilted – even when correct. Consider these examples:

| | | |
|---|---|---|
| Whom did you speak to? | or | Who did you speak to? |
| Whom do you believe? | or | Who do you believe? |
| Whom can it be? | or | Who can it be? |
| Whom did he help? | or | Who did he help? |
| Whom did he marry? | or | Who did he marry? |
| Whom will they choose? | or | Who will they choose? |

Strictly speaking, *whom* is correct in each case because the *who* refers to a third party, i.e. the object. But it would also be overly formal (just like, *With whom did you speak?*). It would be awkward to insist on *whom* in the case of 'whom did she marry?' In truth, modern English speakers prefer to use *who* in cases such as these. Few would go out of their way to insist on using *whom* – even though it is technically correct. Compared with the rest of the contents of this book, the demise of *whom* is not one that I will lose sleep over. Someone once said: "Whom, is doomed."

If you are still reading this chapter, you can probably begin to see that getting *who/whom* correct involves much more than learning a new word and its meaning. If you are still interested to understand this further, I would advise you to do some independent research specifically on the matter of subject versus object.

Whichever approach is right for you, my final piece of advice is to avoid *whom* unless you are confident that it is correct. The fear of making a mistake with *who/whom* can lead to people opting for *whom* thinking that they are playing it safe, only to get it wrong. As a linguistic *faux pas*, using *whom* when it is not needed is far worse than getting it wrong the other way round. If you care about how others will judge your English, then avoid falling into this group. It is amazing how many people do!

# 05

## less versus fewer

*How many fewer? How much less?*

✓ **5 items or fewer.**
✗ *5 items or less.*
✓ **I try to use fewer plastic bags.**
✗ *I try to use less plastic bags.*
✓ **I will try to eat less chocolate.**
✗ *I will try to eat fewer chocolate.*

**Think of *less* in terms of meaning "not as much" and *fewer* as meaning "not as many".**

Getting *less* and *fewer* right isn't always straightforward. If the explanation above does not make immediate sense, ask yourself this question about what it is you want to refer to: would you say, "How many?" or "How much?" Write *fewer* when you would answer "many" and write *less* when you would answer "much".

**EXAMPLE:**

**Items**      How many items?
               *many = fewer*
               ✓ **Five items or fewer**
               ✗ *Five items or less*

**People**     How many people?
               *many = fewer*
               ✓ **There were fewer people than expected**
               ✗ *There were less people than expected*

**Money**      How much money?
               *much = less*
               ✓ **£100 or less**
               ✗ *£100 or fewer*

**Points**     How many points?
*much = less*
✓ **I now have fewer points**
✗ *I now have less points*

You should find it easier to get *less* and *fewer* right by following the simple guidelines above.

Some things, however, can still cause confusion, especially when it comes to *years*, *months*, *hours* and *units of currency*. Ask yourself if the following are correct:

I am working less hours.
She has been with the company three years less than me.
He got paid £200 less than me.
She should be vaccinated at less than 11 months.

All of these sentences are correct because they refer to *a span of time* or *lump sums* – we are talking about "how much time" and "how much money", not necessarily the individual hours or pounds.

Whether or not to write "less doctors", "less teachers" or even "less soldiers" is also a tricky one. Although, technically, these professionals can be lumped together (like *money* and *time*) and seen as a mass or collective group, this approach is generally discouraged because this description tends to dehumanise and devalue each professional's input and the role that they play as individuals. Most people want to be treated by a doctor, not an anonymous, faceless health worker. In return, these professionals prefer to be treated as individuals and for you to use *fewer*.

✓ **The school has decided to employ fewer teachers next year.**
✗ *The school has decided to employ less teachers next year.*
✓ **We were shocked to find out that there are fewer doctors in our area than there used to be.**
✗ *We were shocked to find out that there are less doctors in our area than there used to be.*

The same rules apply to *least* and *fewest*:

✓ **I did not think that I would get the fewest votes of all of the candidates.**
✗ *I did not think that I would get the least votes of all of the candidates.*

This corresponds with our trick of asking *how many* or *how much* votes.

# 06

## redundancies and tautologies
*How much are your free gifts?*

✘ *no added additives*

### Streamline your writing by removing redundant words.

A tautology is saying the same thing twice. A redundant word is one that is unnecessary, like *end result*. Choose your words carefully.

✓ **gift**
✘ *free gift*
✓ **ice**
✘ *frozen ice*
✓ **venom**
✘ *poisonous venom*
✓ **order**
✘ *pre-order*
✓ **fundamentals**
✘ *basic fundamentals*
✓ **bonus**
✘ *added bonus*
✓ **and/also**
✘ *and also*
✓ **monopoly**
✘ *complete monopoly*
✓ **degree**
✘ *university degree*
✓ **HIV**
✘ *HIV virus*
✓ **in August**
✘ *in the month of August*
✓ **postpone**
✘ *postpone until later*
✓ **free**
✘ *for free*
✓ **summary**
✘ *brief summary*
✓ **cameo**
✘ *cameo appearance*

✓ **result**
✘ *end result*
✓ **filled**
✘ *filled to capacity*
✓ **blue**
✘ *blue in colour*
✓ **dilemma**
✘ *difficult dilemma*
✓ **midnight**
✘ *12 midnight*
✓ **alone**
✘ *alone by myself*
✓ **cancel**
✘ *cancel out*
✓ **status**
✘ *current status*
✓ **imports**
✘ *foreign imports*
✓ **truth**
✘ *honest truth*
✓ **exaggerate**
✘ *over exaggerate*
✓ **opposite**
✘ *complete opposite*
✓ **best**
✘ *best ever*
✓ **bouquet**
✘ *bouquet of flowers*
✓ **scrutiny**
✘ *close scrutiny*

✓ **could**
✗ *could possibly*
✓ **depreciate**
✗ *depreciate in value*
✓ **evolve**
✗ *evolve over time*
✓ **tundra**
✗ *frozen tundra*
✓ **witness**
✗ *eyewitness*
✓ **proverb/cliche**
✗ *old proverb/cliche*
✓ **remains**
✗ *still remains*
✓ **goal**
✗ *ultimate goal*
✓ **high**
✗ *high up*
✓ **pure**
✗ *100% pure*
✓ **court**
✗ *courthouse*

✓ **trend**
✗ *current trend*
✓ **estimated at**
✗ *estimated at about*
✓ **colleague/housemate**
✗ *fellow colleague/housemate*
✓ **introduced a**
✗ *introduced a new*
✓ **pending**
✗ *now pending*
✓ **fad**
✗ *passing fad*
✓ **impulse**
✗ *sudden impulse*
✓ **write**
✗ *write down*
✓ **noon**
✗ *12 noon*
✓ **introduced**
✗ *first introduced*
✓ **only**
✗ *one and only*

In my (own) opinion, it is not necessary to write (down) more words than are needed. After (close) scrutiny, I think you will agree that the above list (of redundant words and tautologies) is both amusing and (also) useful. While a lot of people (still) remain who use them (themselves), I hope that you will resist any (sudden) impulse to do the same. This advice is (100%) pure gold.

# 07

## the truth about split infinitives
### *Anyone for a splitting headache?*

✓ **Remember to always wear matching socks.**

**So, what is wrong with split infinitives? Nothing. Every authority on the English language agrees that it is one of the biggest myths of all time.**

> My boss really wants to see better results.
> My boss wants to really see better results.
> Make sure not to get lost.
> Make sure to not get lost.
> I am finally going to be my own boss.
> I am going to finally be my own boss.

The notion of the so-called "split infinitive" deserves serious and critical unpacking because it is, for many, the great taboo in the English language. The prejudice against it is unjustified and the charges are false; if anything, they are trumped up. If you find this to be overly harsh in tone, then you underestimate the level of scorn that is vented by those who are firmly set on keeping this conspiracy theory alive.

According to the so-called "rule", words like *really*, *never*, *deliberately*, *not*, *briefly* etc should not go between *to + verb*. Here are a few examples:

> My boss wants me to <u>really</u> work on my English skills.
> I have made up my mind to <u>never</u> speak to her ever again.
> It is a crime to <u>deliberately</u> avoid paying taxes, as well as to <u>not</u> disclose offshore income.
> It was designed to <u>not</u> look new.
> The team continues to <u>effectively and thoroughly</u> meet their targets.
> The doctor is now going to <u>briefly</u> explain the procedure to you.

For those of you not cringing by now, the underlined words are the "offending" parts of the sentences above. Putting words (adverbs)

20

between *to* + *verb* like this is not allowed. Why not? Because this would supposedly "split" the infinitive verb (*to* + *verb* → *to* + word + *verb*) and cause the word order to be "ungrammatical". Hence, the so-called "rule".

How about one *to* and two verbs? Does that an infinitive spliteth?

> Our goal is to detect and <u>accurately</u> measure changes in behaviour.
> You should already know how to cool and <u>carefully</u> manipulate ice crystals.

You tell me. The truth is that this "rule" is nothing more than a fable. It has been described as a superstition; like not walking under a ladder. So, what should you do? Nothing.

There is nothing wrong with writing and speaking this way. That is all of the advice you need, but read on if you are interested – or because you do not believe me.

If you have never heard of a split infinitive, think yourself lucky; you have lived in bliss until now. A lot of less fortunate people have been trained or taught to avoid using them according to the mistaken view that split infinitives are any and all of the following: "ungrammatical" (not true); "poor English" (not true); "display a lack of education" (hardly); and "ugly", "abhorrent" or "slovenly" (that is just a matter of opinion, like saying that lilac is a horrible colour). I will add "hypercorrect" to this impressive list.

When you ask the same people what they have against split infinitives the answer will always be something along the lines of: "It is bad grammar because Latin infinitives can't be split, therefore it is wrong." When pressed further why this matters and how it relates to English, which does not come from Latin, the answer will usually be something like: "Well, *to* plus *a verb* form the infinitive. And putting a word between them splits them. That is why."

First, forget Latin. The whole argument is false. The Latin justification is a red herring. The split infinitive is actually an erroneous concept.

At the heart of this myth is the idea that *to* somehow belongs to the infinitive – that *to try*, for example, is an infinitive and that any word comes between them – like, say, *really* – will render *to really try* "ungrammatical"; or "split" it. Hence, a "split infinitive". This is not actually true. Look up *infinitive* in the dictionary (or grammar book) and you will find something like:

> **In·fin·i·tive** |in'finitiv| n. the base or basic form of a verb (e.g., *write* in *we want to write a book*).

Note that it reads '*write* in *we want to write a book*' and not '*to write* in *we want to write a book*'. This is an important clue.

So, rather than *to* + *verb* equalling the infinitive, it is just "basic verb equals infinitive". In *to play*, only the word *play* forms the infinitive. The word *to* acts as nothing more than a particle (or infinitive marker, if you prefer); it is not wedded to the verb or the infinitive in any way. The two words are in no way "fused" or inseparable, nor do they form a grammatical bond or unit of any kind. Here are three examples of infinitives (underlined):

| | |
|---|---|
| We need to <u>play</u> well today | We need to really play well today |
| Let's <u>play</u> well today | Let's really play well today |
| They will <u>play</u> well today | They will really play well today |

Putting *really* in front of *play* does not alter the infinitive one bit, regardless of whether there is a *to* there or not. Sure it could come after it, too. Both are fine. All *really* does is give more information about the verb in question – nothing is being "split". So, actually, "split infinitives" are a natural part of English word order (grammar), which is why they occur frequently despite being targeted for eradication over several centuries.

Adverbs sometimes go naturally in front of the verb:

to deliberately avoid paying taxes
to always spell correctly
to mistakenly think
to magically fix

And adverbs sometimes come naturally after the verb:

to walk quietly
to appear suddenly
to act honorably

English is a Germanic language, not a Romance language, one derived from Latin, such as French, Italian and Spanish. The natural word order of Germanic languages is to <u>typically</u> (!) put a "modifier" (anything that adds extra information or acts as a descriptor) in front of the thing, word or phrase that it modifies.

| | |
|---|---|
| to like someone | I want to thank you |
| to really like someone | I want to personally thank you |

For those wanting to avoid a "split infinitive", the only option is to move the adverb somewhere else. However, this will normally do one of two things: change the meaning or sound clunky.

We want you to work really hard this year
= really *describes* hard, *not* work
We want you to really work hard this year
= really *describes* work hard
We really want you to work hard this year
= really *describes* want
We want you to work hard this year, really
= really *means that the speakers are sincere*
We want you really to work hard this year
= really *is in a clunky, unnatural place*

As you can see, the meaning does indeed change. As we know, English relies on word order for meaning and many adverbs typically come directly before the verb.

✓ **Remember to always wear matching socks.**

If *always* moves to the start of the sentence, the instruction is *always remember* rather than *always wear*. Move it anywhere else and the sentence becomes awkward.

Try fixing these examples on your own by shifting the underlined adverbs to another location:

We are concerned that he is going to seriously cause some damage.
This allowed the company to more than double its yearly profits.
The editor was frustrated, waiting for the manuscript to finally come to life.

I am certain that by trying to turn these words round it may take several attempts. You may alternatively be forced to add or rewrite some words (does that *or* count as a split infinitive?). Hopefully you will sense that each attempt will alter, slightly, the meaning.

By moving adverbs elsewhere, the English language is being forced through the Latin model like a round peg through a square hole. Thinking about it too hard just gets messy. Despite the fact that English uses prepositions and Latin uses conjugation to form infinitives, English was forced to imitate Latin – and came out a different shape.

# 09

## different from versus different to/than
### Spot the difference

✓ **Are we really so different from the Victorians?**
✗ *Are we really so different to/than the Victorians?*
✓ **This town seems different from the one I remember growing up in.**
✗ *This town seems different to the one I remember growing up in.*
✗ *This town seems different than the one I remember growing up in.*

**Write *different from* in all formal writing and no one will raise any objections because it is never considered "wrong". If you must, consider restricting *different to* (never *different than*) to informal British English and *different than* (never *different to*) to informal American English.**

The idea that *different from* is the only correct form does not hold water, even if it is enforced by the rules of many publications' house styles. At the same time, the majority of English speakers are probably unaware that there is even any difference between *different from*, *different to* or *different than*. Most will instinctively use one of the three without a second thought about which one they used. If you speak a form of British English you are most likely to use *different to*, and if you use a variety of American English you are likely to use *different than*. Others will use only *different from* because it is considered correct. Using *to* and *than* are seen as either "incorrect", "informal" or "careless". The majority of authorities on English usage confirm this position as false. However, sticking to *from* remains the most favoured and is never wrong.

Each of these three alternatives has long pedigrees. According to the *Oxford English Dictionary*, *different to* dates from 1526, *different from* dates from 1590 and *different than* dates from 1644. Not until the 1900s did strong opinions form, with *different from* gaining broad favour in both the UK and the US. The alternative form *different to* held its own in the UK and *different than* persevered in the US.

Many will put forward a raft of grammatical arguments for why only *from* is correct. Some judge *different than* to be wrong because *different* is not a comparative, but 400 years of continuous usage says otherwise. By contrast, others posit that *than* serves well as a way to avoid awkward repetition in certain constructions and because it invites comparison. Meanwhile, Americans will object to *different to* simply on the basis that it sounds plain wrong – and perhaps because they aren't used to hearing it. It remains a matter of personal preference and, if anything, serves more as a shibboleth.

Here is a summary of the current state of play:

*Different from* – You cannot go wrong with this option because it is the most favoured form on both sides of the Atlantic, especially in formal writing and according to many house styles.

*Different than* – *Different than* is a variant largely restricted to the US. It still largely uncommon in the UK but it is gaining ground thanks to American English. (The common UK variant is *to*.)

*Different to* – Use the variant *different to* only in casual British English and avoid it in US English. Again, some will judge this as incorrect, despite having no problem with indifferent to.

**FORMAL ENGLISH**
✓ **His comments were markedly different from the party line.**
✗ *His comments were markedly different to the party line.*
✗ *His comments were markedly different than the party line.*

**INFORMAL ENGLISH**
✓ **Our circumstances are completely different to theirs (UK).**
✗ *Our circumstances are completely different than theirs (UK).*
✓ **Our circumstances are completely different than theirs (US).**
✗ *Our circumstances are completely different to theirs (US).*

# 10

## while versus whilst / among versus amongst
### *Go straight to gaol*

✓ **While the public has every right to know the details...**
✗ *Whilst the public has every right to know the details...*
✓ **The minister was caught driving while drunk.**
✗ *The minister was caught driving whilst drunk.*
✓ **This device lets you check your e-mail while on holiday.**
✗ *This device lets you check your e-mail whilst on holiday.*
✓ **Enjoy it while it lasts.**
✗ *Enjoy it whilst it lasts.*

**If thou wert wondering what the difference is between** *while* **and** *whilst***, then let me tell thee that thou hast asked the right person.** *While* **is the normal, 21st-century spelling and** *whilst* **is an archaic, regional aberration that refuses to die. Is thine spelling in need of an update?**

Some of you may find the advice in this chapter unsettling. This is because a lot of people have an attachment to *whilst* and *amongst*. American readers will probably skip this chapter because few use *whilst, amongst* etc. Others may find that it sheds light on one of the great mysteries of English usage, namely: what is the difference between using *while* and *whilst*? The answer: nothing, apart from spelling. A good parallel is the word *gaol*. There is nothing "wrong" with using *gaol* because it has a long history and is a legitimate spelling that dates back to Middle English. However, the modern spelling is *jail*. The only difference between them is that one is old and one is new. They both mean the same thing, but using the archaic spelling *gaol* is sure to raise eyebrows and interrupt the reading process in a way that the modern spelling will not. The older spelling looks odd because it is outdated.

The same is true of *while* and *whilst*. Similarly, the four *-st* words *amidst, amongst, unbeknownst* and *whilst* are also older forms of *amid, among, unbeknown* and *while*. These are variants of old regional-dialect forms from a bygone era of the English language that have survived. It is better to stick to the modern forms.

✓ **amid**                    ✓ **among**
✗ *amidst*                    ✗ *amongst*
✓ **unbeknown**               ✓ **while**
✗ *unbeknownst*               ✗ *whilst*

These four words survive only because many people have the belief that they are, let's just say, "more appropriate" than their modern cousins. They are not (this is the uncomfortable part for many). The archaic *-st* forms survive only thanks to the view that they are more "formal", "better" or more "elegant". Neither is strictly incorrect nor correct. As we have seen with many areas of English usage, it is all a matter of style, context and about ensuring consistency. Choosing *amidst/amongst/whilst* over *amid/among/while* is no different from choosing *thou* over *you*. The truth is that *-st* forms enjoy only minority status in modern-day English, with the shorter standard form representing between 8:1 and 10:1 in studies of the British Nation Corpus, according to the *Cambridge Dictionary of English Usage*. (In the US, the ratio is believed to be 1500:1 in favour of modern forms.)

✓ **We are now among the best.**
✗ *We are now amongst the best.*

In certain cases, the insistence of *whilst* over *while* is a mark of the amateur writer. No satisfactory reason (grammatically, phonetically, formality-wise etc.) exists for their continued use. Nothing makes them "formal". The *-st* forms are – to use some clever words of my own – orthographical excrescence, which means "unattractive or superfluous addition or feature", tacked onto the end of *amid*, *among*, *unbeknown* and *while*. Even *unbeknown*, let alone *unbeknownst*, is becoming somewhat awkward and out of place. It never ceases to amaze me when someone insists on *whilst* in the first instance while at the same time insists on *email* over *e-mail* because it is "modern".

Insisting on using the 17th century forms in the 21st century hardly counts as an aspect of modern communications using "good" English. Choosing between *while* and *whilst* is all a matter of style. The truth is that people often insist on *whilst* for pretentious reasons, in the belief that it will make their writing/correspondence more authoritative. A better approach is to look for ways to streamline your writing style by not using a mixture of Middle English and Modern English.

✓ **a marginal fraction**
✓ **a large fraction**
✓ **a huge fraction**

✓ **a limited fraction**
✓ **a significant fraction**

There is a similar amount of prickliness associated with the word *decimate*. The original Latin meaning, "reduce by a tenth" or "taken as a tenth", no longer holds water in modern usage. Its accepted meaning today is "devastate" or "reduce substantially" (often describing some form of unrelenting force), despite grumbles from traditionalists who argue for the restoration of its so-called "literal" meaning. The mathematical meaning is now all but lost. Whether or not this position still has merit, it is a shame in one way because with so many good words for causing destruction, using plain old *decimated* can arguably be considered both understated and unimaginative.

However, now that the genie is out of the bottle, there are several things to look out for with the modern usage of *decimate*.

First, be sure not to use it in ways such as *literally decimated* or *decimated by 80%* because *decimate* is a loose and vague term that is best used on its own. It should not be used together with any expression of "precision".

Second, *decimate* should also not be used in the sense of "destroy completely". The operative meaning remains reduce with ferocity, not kill off in total or make extinct.

✓ **The region's population is being rapidly decimated by disease.**
✗ *The region's entire population is being rapidly decimated by disease.*

Third, having just said the above it is worth noting that American English does allow one dispensation akin to "raze" – homes, villages and cities are said to be *decimated* in the sense of "destroyed in full". This is not (yet) considered correct in British English.

✗ *Chinese town decimated by flood.*

This is to be avoided because the problem is immediate: was it completely wiped out or did some parts of the town remain. This kind of ambiguity is not helpful.

✓ **(US) The remote town was decimated by flood.**
✓ **(UK) The remote town was wiped out by the floods.**

The expression *wiped out* still works best and has a lot of life in it.

Fourth, avoid the newer, most recent, modern interpretation of *decimate*, which uses it as a synonym of *devastate* in terms of "personal loss or tragedy". This should not be encouraged.

✓ **Fans were devastated by the news that he was dead.**
✗ *Fans were decimated by the news that he was dead.*

# 12

## intend to versus intent on
### *I am intent on writing 'intend to'*

✓ **Don't come back unless you intend to apologise first.**
✗ *Don't come back unless you intend on apologising first.*
✓ **How long do you intend to stay?**
✗ *How long do you intend on staying?*
✓ **They all intend to quit smoking this year.**
✗ *They all intend on quitting smoking this year*
✓ **The author is intent on defying her critics.**
✗ *The author is intent to defy her critics.*
✓ **I intend to keep a low profile**
✗ *I intent to keep a low profile.*
✓ **I do not intend to apply.**
✗ *I am not intending to apply.*
✗ *I am not intending on applying.*

**Remember to write *intend to* and *intent on*, not *intend on*. Use *-ing* forms after *intent on* but not after *intend to*.**

There is a common confusion between *intend* and *intent*. Try to avoid using 'intend on' instead of *intend to*. *Intend* is just like you would, for example, *want* or *plan*:

✓ **We want to...**
✓ **We plan to...**
✓ **We intend to...**

✗ *We plan on...*
✗ *We intend on...*

*Intent* means, "having determination" or "being earnest", and is used either on its own or as an adjective. *Intent on* describes the intensity of your action.

✓ **The prosecutor wasn't able to prove intent.**
✗ *The prosecutor wasn't able to prove intend.*

✓ **I am intent on facing my accuser.**
✗ *The inspector gave me an intent look.*

The second, related difference between using *intent on* and *intend to* is how they affect the word coming directly after:

✓ **I am intent on being rich by the time I retire.**
✓ **I intend to be rich by the time I retire.**
✗ *I intend being rich by the time I retire.*

The *intent on* forms have *-ing* forms after it and *intend to* forms do not, as seen above.

A third point to remember is that *intend* – contrary to common belief – does not need the word *for* after it. It is not the end of the world to write *intend for* but it is a point of usage that does annoy some purists.

✓ **I did not intend this to happen.**
✗ *I did not intend for this to happen.*
✓ **The author did not intend such a feeling of sympathy.**
✗ *The author did not intend for such a feeling of sympathy.*

On a final point, a shorter way to write the common phrase *to/for all intents and purposes* is *in effect* or *effectively*.

✓ **What it comes down to, in effect, is money.**
✗ *What it comes down to, for all intents and purposes, is money.*
✓ **The company is effectively bankrupt.**
✗ *The company is to all intents and purposes bankrupt.*

# 13

## a model sentence structure
### *Somebody did something*

**Think of a sentence as being like an arrow or dart. An arrow flies because it is propelled forwards by the weight of its head and is stabilised by its tail. Similarly, a well structured sentence begins with a weighty beginning that carries the remaining words. Good sentences use what I call "somebody did something" as its head; in other words, a subject followed by an active verb. Another analogy is a horse pulling a cart.**

Consider these three sentences:

> The hungry wolves moved south in search of food and water because of the drought.
> In search of food and water, the hungry wolves moved south because of the drought.
> In search of food and water, because of the drought, the hungry wolves moved south.

Note the position of the subject (*the wolves*) and what they do (the verb *move*). Which of these sentences is the clearest? Which is the most direct? All three sentences express the same meaning but in different ways. The second example might be considered good for "story telling" because it employs the "once upon a time" model, but it still has a kink in it – hence the need for commas. The *wolves* are the subject of the sentence, not the *drought*, the *lack of water* or the *search for food*. So why not make the wolves the thrust of the sentence and begin with them? Why put the cart in front of the cart?

Have a look at the number of commas that each sentence requires. The sentence beginning with the wolves first does not require one and is therefore the most streamlined and the easiest to read and comprehend because there is no need for a pause.

Good English also means constructing good sentences. Many writing guides recommend active verbs and comma-free sentences. Nothing makes a reader keep reading than neat sentences that get to the point by employing the 'somebody did something' model. Any other information after who did what is secondary, yet many writers have the habit of starting sentences with secondary information first (for "setting", they say), followed by a comma and then *somebody did something.*

> ✘ *Based on our latest forecast model, which includes all of the relevant data, surveys and up-to-date costs, we recommend going ahead with the project.*
> ✘ *Last year, more chocolate was sold by the company than any time in its 150-year history.*
> ✘ *Last year, the company sold more chocolate than any time in its 150-year history.*

This type of writing can quickly become tedious to read. This is where the "somebody does something" model will help. Let's rewrite these two examples:

> ✓ **The company sold more chocolate last year than any time in its 150-year history.**
> ✓ **We recommend going ahead with the project based on our latest forecast model, which includes all of the relevant data, surveys and up-to-date costs.**

Both sentences are now much better than the first attempt. Writing it in this order will get readers' attention immediately, when they are still alert. This is the beauty of writing active sentences. Here is a handy model to follow:

[description] **somebody** [when] **did something** [because] [and then…].

This might look complicated at first, but the nucleus of this model is – yes, I have mentioned it a few times now – somebody did something. Let's break it down:

The children laughed.
**somebody did something**
The [large group of young] children laughed.
[description] **somebody did something**.

sat on by Humpty-Dumpty". Is the story about a wall? No. That *would* be boring.

Active verbs are great because they keep the focus on who is *doing the doing*. They also portray events in a logical sequence. Who would ever say, "My daughter was married at a wedding yesterday!" A lot of people do write this way. No, it would be, "My daughter got married yesterday!" Once you become attuned to their existence you will begin to see it used everywhere.

Every writer should learn to be aware of the problems that passive verbs introduce. Weeding them out of one's writing is a fast way to better writing. Before you review your own writing, the first step is to learn to recognise them, but they are not always easy to spot.

Some of the telltale signs include words like these:

| | | |
|---|---|---|
| ...was bitten by a dog | → | A dog bit |
| ...has been sent by her | → | She sent... |
| ...you will be informed | → | We will inform you... |
| ...a PDF file is enclosed | → | I/We have enclosed a PDF file... |

Passives are easy to make and are often hard to see, so do not be disheartened if it takes you a while to "get" the concept. The process may require patience and practice, but keep working at it and do not give up. I can almost guarantee that you will not be the only one scratching you head at first. (See also **76**.)

# 15

## that (the omission of)
### *How could you forget 'that'?*

✓ **There is no denying that you need urgent help.**
✗ *There is no denying you need urgent help.*
✓ **The problem is that the goalposts keep moving.**
✗ *The problem is the goalposts keep moving.*
✓ **This is the first time that Paul has confided in me.**
✗ *This is the first time Paul has confided in me.*

**Try not to forget the so-called "clause connector" *that*.
Take care to include this in your writing and it will retain
a greater degree of clarity, as well as be more suited to
formal contexts.**

The word *that* has been described as the workhorse of the English language
because it has so many uses. This chapter is specifically concerned with
when it can and when it is best not omitted.

In private conversations we often speed up communications by paring
away our words and using contractions. We aren't concerned with
formality when we speak to our friends, but when it comes to formal
contexts (e-mails, speeches, reports, application letters etc.) we have to be
on our toes and use whole words and complete sentences.

One thing that often gets overlooked is *that* when it links two clauses
in a sentence – which functions as a bridge between clauses – hence the
name "clause connector" (the proper name is *conjunction*).

✓ **The score was level at half-time and both teams knew that
history would be made in the second half.**
✗ *The score was level at half-time and both teams knew history would
be made in the second half.*
✓ **It cannot be denied that more should be done to improve
literacy standards across the country.**
✗ *It cannot be denied more should be done to improve literacy
standards across the country.*

First, it is good practice to always include *that* when it acts as a "clause connector", similar to the way that *and* links sentences and clauses.

A lot of people skip *that* in informal, spoken English, but formal English requires it. In the same way that there exists a school of thought that argues that punctuation only gets in the way and slows the reader down. Similarly, another school of thought regards the "clause connector" (conjunction) *that* as unnecessary. They argue (that) sentences become shorter, sharper and neater when *that* is removed. I am not convinced. The danger with regularly removing *that* from your writing is that 'neater' can lead to misunderstanding by the reader, as well as halting the reader's flow. This can create clunky sentences. This headline appeared in a newspaper at the time of writing this book:

> Not the G8 leaders wanted

My guess is that it took you at least two goes to comprehend its meaning and context properly. It would no doubt have been better written as "(This was) not the G8 (that) leaders wanted". Taking care to include *that* in the right places will make your writing instantly more legible.

As you have seen, stripping out the conjunction *that* in this way from sentences is common in reports from media organisations – in both the UK and the US. It can make sense when words take up valuable airtime and column inches. Removing them also makes for a more casual style. But omitting *that* can also lead to unnecessary jarring.

> It took until today to understand what got lost in the translation was actually more important and relevant than I had first realised.
> It took until today to understand that what got lost in the translation was actually more important and relevant than I had first realised.

Do you see how the first sentence, without the all-important *that*, causes the reader's flow to halt briefly when they have to self-correct their train of thought? This may seem like a minor point to worry about but you will do your audience a great service if you keep *that* in. Moreover, a formal audience will expect it.

Now that you have understood this, there are some exceptions. First, *that* can be left out of certain types of sentence. The first of these is when *that* follows directly after what can be described as "mental verbs" such as *know*, *think*, *wish* etc., and "non-physical verbs" such as *feel*, *sense* etc.

I think (that) we should reconsider our position on this and request another meeting.
I wish (that) we could afford to move abroad.
I feel (that) it is time to take our relationship to the next level.
I sense (that) you are unhappy with our relationship.

In these types of sentences it is standard practice and perfectly acceptable to omit *that* – but you can just as well leave them in. Just be aware of the structure because some words, such as *know* and *feel*, can be ambiguous.

I felt your presence...
I felt that your presence...
I know what you said...
I know that what you said...

Leaving *that* out can cause the reader to change their understanding mid-way through the sentence because of the changed meaning demonstrated above, especially in long sentences. It just shows how the omission alters the meaning.

Second, it is also standard practice to omit *that* in reported speech after *said*, *says* and *thinks*, but not after *agrees*, *claims* or *insists*.

✓ **He said it was the best thing that had ever happened to him.**
✓ **They say it is all an elaborate hoax and that all will be revealed soon.**

This last example also demonstrates how leaving out *that* avoids repeating that twice in a sentence, which is not ideal (*they claim that that is unfair*). On the other hand, *that* should be kept when making a direct reference to a statement.

✓ **You said that, in effect, you are better than everyone else in your department.**

Third, in formal English (such as in business and academia) it remains good practice to retain *that* after these same verbs, especially after words such as *assume*, *believe*, *contend*, *doubt*, *propose* and *suggest* etc.

✓ **The panel felt that you weren't truly committed to your role.**
✓ **We assume that you are interested in a management position.**
✓ **I therefore propose that individuals be required to wear safety equipment.**

✓ **Is it your contention that your proposal is unique in some way?**

Fourth, avoid having to write *that that* by rewriting sentences, not by omitting one of them:

✓ **I did hear that it was pointless.**
✗ *I did hear that that was pointless.*
✓ **We decided that this was the area we wanted to work in.**
✗ *We decided that that was the area we wanted to work in.*

Last, do not omit *that* from expressions such as *so that*, *now that*, *such that* etc. if you do not intend to be informal.

What are you going to do now (that) you are married?

Overall, the philosophy to keep in mind is this: take care to decide where and when to fade between formality and informality in your writing. The inclusion of *that* can be a significant marker of where your level of formality lies. Be sure to include *that* where is deemed appropriate, and there is nothing wrong with erring on the side of caution because it does no harm to always keep it in.

# 16

## in order to/in order that versus to
### *Don't give me any orders*

✓ **We bought a smaller car to save on costs and emissions.**
✗ *We bought a smaller car in order to save on costs and emissions.*
✓ **The government introduced the new laws to save lives.**
✗ *The government introduced the new laws in order to save lives.*

**For plain English, replace *in order to* and *so as to* with *to* and *in order that* with *so that*.**

Having just looked at the omission of *that* (see **15**), now we turn to unnecessary words. Another bad habit is the constant inclusion of *in order (to)*, which is a lot like *very* (see **01**) – it adds nothing.

> We are going to our favourite restaurant to celebrate our anniversary.
> We are going to our favourite restaurant in order to celebrate our anniversary.
> Pay now to avoid any penalty charges.
> Pay now in order to avoid any penalty charges.
> I only did it to help you.
> I only did it in order to help you.

The words *in order to* and *so as to* are in no way different in meaning from plain, old *to*. Both mean the same thing and serve exactly the same function.

Another thing that can happen is unwanted ambiguity with *in order* (for example, *smallest to largest*).

> The topics are selected in order to explain the whole process.
> Make sure to interview everyone in order to be thorough.

This kind of writing can cause confusion for readers. Does the writer intend *in order to* or just *in order*? Your guess is as good as mine. The good news is that a simple fix will solve the problem: just remove *in order*.

So why then, does it crop up everywhere?

✓ **We did \_\_\_\_ to \_\_\_\_.**
✗ *We did \_\_\_\_ so as to \_\_\_\_.*
✗ *We did \_\_\_\_ in order to \_\_\_\_.*

so as to     →     to
in order to     →     to

Second, the variant *in order that* can be shortened to *so that*.

✓ **We did \_\_\_\_ so that \_\_\_\_.**
✗ *We did \_\_\_\_ in order that \_\_\_\_.*

in order that     →     so that

Again, there is no difference between the two meanings – only length.

Third is the less important – and arguably archaic – grammatical rule that states: *in order that* can be followed only by the hypothetical *may*, *might*, *sometimes*, *shall* or *should*. According to this unfamiliar rule, it is considered wrong to use the more definite alternatives *can*, *could*, *will* or *would*. Some examples are outlined below:

✓ **We are doing this in order that the underprivileged may/might benefit from our programme.**
✗ *We are doing this in order that the underprivileged will benefit from our programme.*
✗ *We are doing this in order that the underprivileged can benefit from our programme.*

Whether you choose to follow, or remember, this last rule is another matter. I do not imagine that too many will notice or object when this peculiar rule is broken. Nonetheless, using *to* and *so that* avoids any such problem anyway, so you can use what you like.

✓ **We are doing this so that the underprivileged can benefit from our programme.**

# 17

## adviser versus advisor
### *An adviser provocateur*

✓ **How to choose a financial adviser.**
✗ *How to choose a financial advisor.*
✓ **Medical adviser**
✓ **Legal adviser**
✓ **Policy adviser**

**Many people don't realise that this word has two spellings: the preferred spelling is *adviser* in both British and American English. *Advisor* remains a deviant, second choice for both.**

Unlike *supervisor*, *administrator* and *advisory*, a person who gives advice is an *adviser*. It isn't necessarily wrong to write *advisor* but if you are writing for publication there is a good chance that it will be edited anyway. The key is to maintain consistency if more than one person is contributing to the publication.

# 18

## lose versus loose

*How to loose friends and infuriate people*

✓ **I do not want him to lose faith in me.**
✗ *I do not want him to loose faith in me.*
✓ **Don't lose your keys.**
✗ *Don't loose your keys.*
✓ **I feel like such a loser.**
✗ *I feel like such a looser.*

**Avoid making the surprisingly common mistake of confusing *lose* with *loose*. The opposite of *win* is *lose* and the opposite of *tight* is *loose*.**

✓ **My trousers are a lot looser these days.**
✗ *My trousers are a lot loser these days.*
✓ **My pockets are full of loose change.**
✗ *My pockets are full of lose change.*

There are enough people who make this basic mistake that it deserves to have a chapter of its own. Be careful to spell *lose* correctly.

| ✓ **lose** | ✓ **loser** | ✓ **losing** |
| ✗ *loose* | ✗ *looser* | ✗ *loosing* |

# 19

## its versus it's
### *It's a common problem*

✓ **It is almost midnight.**
✓ **It's almost midnight.**
✗ *Its almost midnight.*
✓ **The dog chased its tail.**
✗ *The dog chased it's tail.*
✓ **Hollywood loses its sparkle.**
✗ *Hollywood loses it's sparkle.*

**If you find it a struggle to get *its* and *it's* right, then one simple way to solve this enigmatic riddle is to banish *it's* from your writing altogether. (Remember that the apostrophe in *it's* denotes the missing *i* in *is*, not "belonging to".) Adopting this technique would leave you only ever having to write one of these two:**

It's  = it is
Its   = belonging to it

✓ **it is**
✓ **its**

If you think of *its* and *it's* his way, if you stick only to *it is* (for "it is") and *its* (for any other meaning) then you are more than likely to get it right every time. This will also help imprint in your mind the difference between the two.

Once you are comfortable with the strategy of *it is* and *its* then the only other thing that you need to know is that *it's* – should you decide to use it – is a contraction (see **20**) like *he's* (*he is*) or *there's* (*there is*). If you follow the advice on avoiding contractions in writing overall then this tough nut might never be a problem again.

Not using *because* can also be interpreted as a sign of evasiveness or that the writer is uncertain.

> As the world turns.
> As the world is overheating.
> Because the world is overheating.

Note that *as* is not strictly incorrect in all circumstances, but part of what being a good writer means is choosing your words with care.

> The children looked on as the ducks swam past.
> The children were scared because the swan came too close.
> We lost the account as our products were not competitive enough.
> We lost the account because our products were not competitive enough.

By using *as* to mean, "while" and not "for the reason", these writers achieve a level of clarity that avoids ambiguity and ultimately improves the writing for their readers (see also **25**).

# 24

## since versus because
*Not since you got here*

✓ **This realisation has always been unpleasant because people stubbornly want to believe in this half-truth.**
✗ *This realisation has always been unpleasant, since people stubbornly want to believe in this half-truth.*

**Careful writers restrict *since* to mean, "from/in the period since" and use *because* to mean, "cause" or "reason".**

Although some dictionaries recognise *since* as sometimes sharing the same territory as *because*, it frequently causes a degree of ambiguity:

> I have been so happy because I finally met you.
> I have been so happy since I finally met you.
> Since global capitalism was unleashed in earnest in the late 1980s, we have seen number of huge systemic shocks.
> Because global capitalism was unleashed in earnest in the late 1980s, we have seen number of huge systemic shocks.

Does the writer mean, *because* or *since*? The second example is more likely to be *since*, but the first example could be either – it is up to the writer to express what they mean correctly. This kind of indiscriminate switching is all too common.

These two sentences illustrate how the intended meaning can be misinterpreted.

✓ **I haven't spoken to you since you lost your job.**
✗ *I haven't spoken to you because you lost your job.*

Clearly, there is a difference. Therefore, writers should restrict *since* to mean, "in the time since" and review their writing for instances where it should be turned into *because*.

The second difference is that writers typically precede *since* with a comma – a comma that is not necessary when using *because*.

✓ **We did it because it had never been done before.**
✗ *We did it, since it had never been done before.*

By sticking to *because* in this way you save a comma and leave *since* to do what it does best: refer to an intervening period of time.

✓ **The coldest weather since records began.**
✓ **Since when have you listened to hip-hop music?**
✓ **This is the first fall in house prices since June.**

# 25

## due to versus because
### *Because it was due for a change*

✓ **My 11.30 patient is due.**
✓ **The next train is due to arrive shortly.**
✓ **The business went under because of financial problems.**
✗ *The business went under due to financial problems.*
✓ **The plane is delayed because of strong head winds.**
✗ *The plane is delayed due to strong head winds.*

## Prefer *because* over *due to* for "cause" or "reason".

It is common in casual English to use *due* instead of *because*. As we have seen in the two earlier chapters (see **23** and **24**), because is sidelined all too often. Careful writers, however, adopt a more precise view of restricting their use of *due to* to mean, "expected". When they need to express "cause/caused by" or "reason" they choose *because*.

The word *due* has many meanings. Strictly speaking, it is a synonym of *owe/owed* (I am due/owed some money) and used as an adjective. It also means, "expected", as well as "proper", "directly", "charge" and "fee":

You will find out in due course. ("proper")
We sailed due south. ("directly")
My train is due to arrive shortly. ("expected")
You haven't paid your dues. ("fees")

With so many meanings already, why assign *due* yet another one, when *because* already does this job perfectly?

Like *as* and *because*, paying close attention to your choice of words will deliver clarity, make your writing more precise and less ambiguous. If you are still not convinced, imagine the following scenario if you don't think it makes a difference:

Q: "Why do you love me?"  →   A: "Due to..."

Nobody says, "I love you due to..." They say, "I love you because..."

# 26

## reason versus reason why

### *No more than one reason why*

✓ **The reason I called is...**

✗ *The reason I called is because...*

✓ **I called because...**

✓ **The reason I chose to study in France was to learn French.**

✗ *The reason I chose to study in France was because I wanted to learn French.*

✓ **I chose to study in France because I wanted to learn French.**

✓ **Tell me the reason.**

✗ *Tell me the reason why.*

✓ **The reason we came to this decision is...**

✓ **The reason that this happened is...**

✗ *The reason why this happened is...*

✓ **The boss wants to know why this month's sales figures are down.**

✗ *The boss wants to know the reason why this month's sales figures are down.*

**Remove either *the reason* or *because* when they appear in the same sentence, and don't write *reason why*.**

Like many redundancies and tautologies (see **06**), we do not notice them until they get pointed out to us. Here is one that you may not have realised before.

✗ *The reason why is because...*

This is a triple tautology. *Because* means "for the reason that". *Reason* means "because" and *why* can also mean, "because/the reason". This is repetition of extreme proportions. Either one of *reason*, *why* or *because* will do on its own, so there is no need to use them all three in the same sentence:

✗ *The reason that I chose to study abroad was because I wanted to learn the language.*

All that needs to be done is, either remove *the reason that* or replace *because* with *that*. This can be cut to:

✓ **I chose to study abroad because I wanted to learn the language.**
✓ **The reason that I chose to study abroad was to learn the language.**

Omitting *the reason* is also usually the better choice because it frames the statement in a direct, active voice. Or, just say what you mean directly without stating it as a reason:

✓ **I chose to study abroad to learn the language.**

The second common mistake to point out is that the word after *reason* should not be *why*, it should be *that* – as in *the reason is that...* Otherwise you are still using the tautologous *reason* and *why*.

✓ **The reason that we came to this decision is...**
✗ *The reason why we came to this decision is...*
✗ *The supervisor wants to know the reason why this month's sales are down.*
✓ **The supervisor wants to know why this month's sales are down.**
✓ **The supervisor wants to know the reason for this month's sales being down.**

Here, *reason* means the same thing and serves the same function as *why*. You might argue that you simply prefer *why*, but like *because*, it also plays the same function as *reason*. Again, it is a case of redundant words that careful writers know to remove.

# 27

## in contrast to versus by contrast
*A lesson in comparing and contrasting*

✓ **By contrast, this year's event was a complete success.**
✗ *In contrast, this year's event was a complete success.*
✓ **In contrast to beer, cider is a much sweeter drink.**
✗ *By contrast to beer, cider is a much sweeter drink.*
✓ **Dave, by contrast, doesn't agree with the plan.**
✗ *Dave, in contrast, doesn't agree with the plan.*

**Write *in contrast to*, without commas, followed directly by your comparison. Always use commas with *by contrast*, followed by your contrasting statement.**

Many writers make indiscriminate use of *in contrast* and *by contrast* without considering what each of them does.

To begin with, *by contrast* often appears at the beginning of a sentence followed directly by a comma, and then a contrasting point of view or statement:

✓ **By contrast, Britain comes to a grinding halt every time there is snow.**
✗ *In contrast, Britain comes to a grinding halt every time there is snow.*

A sentence like this will typically be making a comparison with a previous sentence, statement or paragraph. *By contrast* can also be inserted between commas. This technique is used as a form of reminder:

✓ **The Aussies, by contrast, kept their nerve and focused on the task at hand: getting wickets.**
✗ *The Aussies by contrast kept their nerve and focused on the task at hand: getting wickets.*
✗ *The Aussies, in contrast, kept their nerve and focused on the task at hand: getting wickets.*

By contrast, *in contrast to* (not *with*) needs no commas and is directly followed by the example being given as a comparison. It can be used to start a sentence or in the middle of one.

✓ **In contrast to his public persona, he was an immensely private person.**

✗ *In contrast he was an immensely private person, and different from his public persona.*

✓ **The latest results are in contrast to analysts' expectations.**

✓ **And, in contrast to public opinion, Britain does not actually have a shortage of housing.**

# 28

## should have versus 'should of'
### *Woulda-shoulda-coulda*

✓ **He should have called by now.**
✓ **He should've called by now.**
✗ *He should of called by now.*

✓ **May have/may not have**
✗ *May of/may not of*
✓ **Could have/could not have**
✗ *Could of/could not of*
✓ **Should have/should not have**
✗ *Should of/should not of*
✓ **Might have/might not have**
✗ *Might of/might not of*
✓ **Must/must not have**
✗ *Must of/must not of*
✓ **Would have/would not have**
✗ *Would of/would not of*

**Be sure to write *should have*, *might have* etc., never *should of* or *might of* etc.**

A surprising number of people incorrectly write *of* instead of *have* after *could*, *should*, *may*, *might*, *must*, *would* etc. This comes across as careless English and should be avoided at all costs, especially if you are writing to your boss, for publication or to your clients.

In spoken English, of course, *should've* sounds like "should of", which is where this error comes from. Regardless of how you choose to say it, take care to always write it correctly.

✓ **You should have listened to Max and Stacey.**
✗ *You should of listened to Max and Stacey.*

# 29

## were versus was

### *I would not do that if I were you*

✓ **If I were in charge I would do things differently.**
✗ *If I was in charge I would do things differently.*
✓ **I would not do that if I were you.**
✗ *I would not do that if I was you.*

**It is standard practice – especially in formal writing – to use *were* instead of *was* to express hypothetical statements and impossible or imagined situations.**

The mistake to avoid is using *was* instead of the correct form *were*. Unlike *I was* and *we were* (i.e. when *were* is used in the plural past tense) *were* is also used to express hypothetical, conditional or imagined statements.

✓ **If I were a teenager again.**
✗ *If I was a teenager again.*
✓ **Were I to accept your offer, I would need it in writing.**
✗ *If I was to accept your offer, I would need it in writing.*
✓ **If only she were rich.**
✗ *If only she was rich.*
✓ **Just imagine if it were really true!**
✗ *Just imagine if it was really true!*

In spoken English, using *were* (used correctly) can come across as overly formal, so it is common to say *was* in casual conversation. That said, this is not considered correct, so care must be taken to use it correctly when circumstances require it.

Remember, too, that *was* is required when circumstances are allegedly true:

✓ **If she was at her desk, then how could her computer have been stolen?**
✗ *If she were at her desk, then how could her computer have been stolen?*

# 30

## that versus which
### *Not the every which way*

✓ **The key is to write something that is clear.**
✗ *The key is to write something which is clear.*
✓ **I work in an industry that only recruits the brightest.**
✗ *I work in an industry which only recruits the brightest.*
✗ *I work in an industry, which only recruits the brightest.*
✓ **Technology changes constantly, which makes it hard to keep up.**
✗ *Technology changes constantly that makes it hard to keep up.*

**The two golden rules to live by are: write *that* when no comma is needed; and *which* when a comma is needed. The exceptions are in the constructions *about which*, *in which*, *for which* etc. or when *which* starts a sentence.**

> They are keen to see a system which is far.
> They are keen to see a system that is fair.
> The government warned of the large cuts which we face.
> The government warned of the large cuts that we face.

Is there a difference between the two sets of sentences above? Are any of them right or wrong? Is one better than the other?

This is the only chapter in this book where slightly more grammatical explanation is required. Read on to find out more.

Essentially, that and which are used in two particular types of sentence structure. (Of course, there are more, but this chapter concerns the "that versus which" dilemma.) In one, that and which are arguably interchangeable; in the other, they are not.

> Hospital trusts which are failing must be closed immediately.
> Hospital trusts that are failing must be closed immediately.

Let's look a little closer. The first type of sentence looks like this:

> The client asked for a product that will sell.

70

The client asked for a product which will sell.

This sentence can be broken down into two parts:

The client asked for a product    +    that will sell.

The second half (*that will sell*) relates directly to and describes the first half because "a product that will sell" is what the client asked for. Not any old "product". More specifically, the words "that will sell" are absolutely necessary because they *define* "product" – not just *describe* it.

This is known as a "restrictive clause" in the UK and a "defining clause" in the US. I am going to call it an "essential *that*".

Now, let's now look at the second type of sentence structure in question:

He turned to religion, <u>which</u> gave him the strength to continue.

Here, the words after *which* are not, by contrast, directly necessary in defining "religion". What they instead do is simply provide additional information and context. In other words, the words after *which* play no role in defining "religion". He did not turn to "a religion *that* gave him the strength to continue", instead he simply turned to *religion*, and by doing so it later gave him strength.

This type of sentence is known as a "non-restrictive clause" in the UK and a "non-defining clause" in the US. I am going to call it a "non-essential *which*".

    ✓ **Books are the best data-storage devices that have been devised.**
    ✗ *Books are the best data-storage devices which have been devised.*
    ✓ **The new kitchen, which cost a fortune, makes my wife happy.**
    ✗ *The new kitchen that cost a fortune makes my wife happy.*
    ✗ *The new kitchen which cost a fortune makes my wife happy.*

This type of sentence must use a comma. There is no option to use *that*. Only *which* is applicable here.

So, in summary, *that* is used for clauses where the words coming after it are essential to the meaning of the statement. And *which*, always preceded by a comma, is used for clauses that are non-essential to the meaning of the statement and instead provides additional information.

### "ESSENTIAL THAT"
✓ **I went to a school that was multicultural.**
✗ *I went to a school which was multicultural.*
✓ **This was the best thing that could have happened.**
✗ *This was the best thing which could have happened.*
✓ **There are still some questions that need to be answered.**
✗ *There are still some questions which need to be answered.*
✓ **The country is still in recession, according to a report that measured key metrics.**
✗ *The country is still in recession, according to a report which measured key metrics.*

### "NON-ESSENTIAL WHICH"
✓ **This produced strange patterns, which the scientists photographed and logged.**
✗ *This produced strange patterns that the scientists photographed and logged .*
✓ **He wrote *The Joy of English*, which was written in just one month.**
✗ *He wrote* The Joy of English *that was written in just one month.*
✓ **He started the group, which now has 10,000 members.**
✗ *He started the group that now has 10,000 members.*

This is the system put forward by Fowler in the 1920s. Major publishers, institutions and professional writers have since adopted it because of the clarity that it lends writing. The authoritative *Chicago Manual of Style*, an important reference work in the US, also backs this system. It is also why MS Word underlines *which* when it breaks this rule.

Now, some of you may well be reaching for your grammar books and are looking in the index for 'relative pronouns', 'that versus which' or 'restrictive/non-restrictive clauses', eager to point out the section that reads along the lines of, 'it makes no difference whether or not you use that or which'. What you must remember is that this advice relates only to "essential clauses" (restrictive) but does not apply to "non-essential clauses" (non-restrictive).

Others may also be thinking to themselves, "Well, I always thought *which* was better and more formal than *that*. That's how I was taught to use it at my grammar school." But the view that *which* is somehow better/grander/superior to *that* is, to quote the BBC's *News Style Guide* for journalists, 'complete rot'. When it comes to "essential clauses", both are equally valid – but only one is preferred.

Astute readers will protest that I just contradicted myself. You might be asking, "but if they are both acceptable, why can't I just use *which*?" The answer is – and this is the necessity of Fowler's system – if we all use *which* for "essential" as well as "non-essential" clauses, then everything becomes *which* and a large degree of clarity and meaning is immediately lost. Here are some examples that I found on the BBC's website:

> This watch was used by a guard on trains which travelled on the old Strawberry Line, which was part of Somerset and Dorset railway.

> This is the piece of UK legislation which tells you which incidents have to be reported to the authorities.

The problem with choosing *which* over *that* with sentences of this type is that you end up using *which* with everything. The structure becomes clumsy and difficult to read, as well as its double use of *which*. Fowler's system clears up it immediately, by assigning separate functions to *that* and *which*.

✓ **This watch was used by a guard on trains that travelled on the old Strawberry Line, which was part of Somerset and Dorset railway.**
✓ **This is the piece of UK legislation that tells you which incidents have to be reported to the authorities.**

This system also helps remove ambiguity when it arises:

> The report recommends changes in the law that would enable consumers to avoid high fees.
> The report recommends changes in the law, which would enable consumers to avoid high fees.
> He bought the Gucci suit that made him feel really smart.
> He bought the Gucci suit, which made him feel really smart.
> She loved books that gave her a lot of inspiration.
> She loved books, which gave her a lot of inspiration.
> They are staying at the hotel that I booked for them.
> They are staying at the hotel, which I booked for them.

All of these sentence pairs have different meanings – subtle variation that are crystallised by the precise use of *that* and *which* according to this great method. The added beauty of these tools is that they work equally well in spoken English as they do in writing.

Those who remain insistent on using *which* may try to argue that *which* can be used without a comma in "essential clauses" and with one in "non-essential clauses", but the only problem with this is that many writers fail to use the comma correctly on the first place. This brings me to the final mistake to avoid: don't forget the comma before *which*:

> ✓ **The traffic in town was awful, which is why I am so late.**
> ✗ *The traffic in town was awful which is why I am so late.*
> ✓ **It only cost me a fiver, which I can claim back anyway.**
> ✗ *It only cost me a fiver which I can claim back anyway.*

The next tool to remember: there is no need for a preceding comma with the following constructions (and, obviously, no comma is need when *which* begins a sentence):

> ✓ **with which**          ✓ **in which**
> ✓ **for which**          ✓ **to which**
> ✓ **at which**          ✓ **without which**

I hope that I have demonstrated that *which* and *that* certainly are not interchangeable, that *which* is not in fact better than *that* after all. I also hope that you can see the logic and genius of Fowler's system. If you do choose to adopt it – it is, after all, a matter of style and not any form of rule – you will find that you will inject a great deal of both clarity and professionalism to your writing. It will not take you long to appreciate others who do the same.

# 31

## every day versus everyday

*We deal with everyday problems every day*

✓ **I drink everyday wine.**
✗ *I drink every day wine.*
✓ **I drink wine every day.**
✗ *I drink wine everyday.*

✓ **All day, every day.**
✗ *All day everyday.*
✓ **I drive in an everyday car.**
✗ *I drive in an every day car.*

*Every day* **means "daily" and is always written as two words. Use** *everyday* **to describe things that are common or frequent.**

You are not alone if you make the mistake of getting *everyday* and *every day* the wrong way round. This error can be seen on signs, advertisements, menus and posters up and down the country.

A good way to remember them – now that you are aware of the difference – is to think of the phrase "each and every day"; remove the first two words and they still mean, *every day*.

✓ **Fresh food served (each and) every day.**
✓ **I drive a car to work (each and) every day.**
✓ **Fresh food served every day.**
✓ **I drive a car to work every day.**
✗ *Fresh food served everyday.*
✗ *I drive a car to work everyday.*

That leaves the other one, *everyday*, which is used in place of "ordinary".

✓ **everyday life**
✗ *every day life*
✓ **everyday job**
✗ *every day job*

✓ **everyday house**
✗ *every day house*
✓ **everyday person**
✗ *every day person*

(For more about joined-up words, see also **44**, **52**, **53**, **54**, **81**, **63** and **90**.)

# 32

## over versus more than
### *The play continued over 10 years*

✓ **I sold more than 80 pairs of shoes.**
✗ *I sold over 80 pairs of shoes.*
✓ **The vandals caused more than £1000 of damage.**
✗ *The vandals caused over £1000 of damage.*

**Consider using *more than* instead of *over* for "in excess of" with numbers. It is not wrong to use *over* but there is a strong bias in formal English towards *more than*.**

I have been here more than 5 years.
I have been here over 5 years.
We want to fly over 100 people in our aeroplane.
We want to fly more than 100 people in our aeroplane.

Many voices argue that *over* should not be used to mean, *more than*. This thinking is based on the idea of associating *over* with the physical sense "over(head)" (to fly over [above] 100 people in an aeroplane) and adopting *more than* for "in excess of" (to fly more than 100 people in an aeroplane). It perhaps stems from there being many meanings of *over*. In dictionary terms, *over* has no fewer than 60 or so meanings.

Nonetheless, the use of *over* in the numerical (*more than*) way remains perfectly good Germanic English – having been in usage since the 1300s. There is nothing wrong with it, despite the prejudice against it. Its use came under criticism in the US during the late 1800s, but not in the UK, where it continued to be Standard English. It wasn't until the early 1900s that this view took hold in the UK.

While writing *over £100* is perfectly legitimate according to usage authorities, bear in mind that many house-style requirements and publishing professionals may insist that you use *more than*, for "precision's sake". Writer and journalist Theodore Bernstein called it a "superstition" in his books on English usage. As he points out, no one ever has a problem with *under £100*.

Now that you are aware of *more than* versus *over*, you will probably notice how prevalent the former is in the media now and you may become more inclined to use it, too.

One area of possible ambiguity associated with *over* is with its other meaning of "duration over time".
Compare the following:

> The diplomatic wrangling continued in secrecy over 50 years.
> This film will not interest people over 50 years.
> The band will play over 18 nights.

This last one does not mean, "more than 18 nights" but "over the course of 18 nights". This one is reason that *more than* suits "in excess of", confining *over* to a separate meaning.

There is one final point about *more than*, namely the subtle distinction between writing *for more than* and *in more than*:

> ✓ **I have not seen Paul for more than a year.**
> ✗ *I have not seen Paul in more than a year.*

This might come as a surprise to some, but the 'in more than' form is no longer considered correct. It was the correct preposition between the 1400s and the 1800s to express a period of time in negative statements of this type. *For* has since replaced it. Sometimes it is obvious:

> ✓ **My father refused to speak to me for more than a month.**
> ✗ *My father refused to speak to me in more than a month.*

Sometimes it is not:

> ✓ **This level of skill has not been witnessed for more than a decade.**
> ✗ *This level of skill has not been witnessed in more than a decade.*
> ✓ **I have not been out of the house for 48 hours.**
> ✗ *I have not been out of the house in 48 hours.*

Don't confuse *in just over* with *for more than*, which convey separate meanings.

> ✓ **I will be gone for more than a month.**
> ✓ **I will be gone in just over a month.**
> ✓ **We went out for more than 3 years.**
> ✓ **We are getting married in just over 3 months.**

# 33

## male/female versus men's/women's
### *I am seeing a female locker room*

✓ **Men's toilets**
✗ *Male toilet*
✓ **Women's clothes**
✗ *Female clothes*
✓ **He oozes masculine beauty.**
✗ *He oozes male beauty.*
✓ **I demand to see a female doctor.**
✗ *I demand to see a woman doctor.*
✓ **Women's cancers**
✗ *Female cancers.*

**Use *male/female* to say what gender something is; use *masculine/feminine* to describe the attributes of people or things; and *men's* or *women's* for "belonging to" or "intended for".**

*Female* and *male* denotes the gender type of a species – a biological, living organism able to exchange genes and breed with its opposite equivalent to produce offspring. In other words, living things of either gender.

✗ *Buy two male tickets and get one free.*

Inanimate objects cannot be given the adjective male or female because they cannot reproduce. It is like referring to a product for women as *she* rather than *it*. There are no such things as *male toilets* and *female cancers*. Likewise, it is incorrect to write: *female clothes*, *male problems* or *female hairstyles*.

Male and *female* typically describe types of people when it is necessary to mention their gender: *male doctor*, *female author* and *male holiday-makers*. The use of *female* to mean, *woman* is also to be avoided, such as in *single, white female*.

For things that typically belong to or affect either sex, *men's* or *women's* should be used.

✓ **women's issues**      ✓ **women's rights**
✓ **women's minds**      ✓ **women's shoes**
✓ **women's prisons**

✓ **men's fashion**      ✓ **men's magazines**
✓ **men's grooming**      ✓ **men's attitudes**
✓ **men's problems**

If you want to give inanimate objects male and female qualities, it is best to use *masculine* and *feminine*.

✓ **men's beauty products**      ✓ **men's feminine sides**
✗ *male beauty products*      ✗ *male feminine sides*
✓ **feminine colours**      ✓ **feminine touch**
✗ *female colours*      ✗ *female touch*
✓ **feminine looks**      ✓ **feminine qualities**
✗ *female looks*      ✗ *female qualities*
✓ **masculine world**      ✓ **masculine beauty**
✗ *male world*      ✗ *male beauty*
✓ **masculine nature**      ✓ **masculine-sounding voice**
✗ *male nature*      ✗ *male-sounding voice*

American readers may be confused about this chapter, wondering why it should be included. That is because the problem of inanimate objects with apparent gender is more prevalent in the UK.

# 35

## full stops
### *Just get straight to the point*

| | |
|---|---|
| ✓ **Inc** | ✓ **Corp** |
| ✗ *Inc.* | ✗ *Corp.* |
| ✓ **UK** | ✓ **EU** |
| ✗ *U.K.* | ✗ *E.U.* |
| ✓ **Ltd** | ✓ **US** |
| ✗ *Ltd.* | ✗ *U.S./U.S.A.* |

**While it is standard to always include *full stops* for abbreviations in American English this is generally not the case in British English, where standard practice is to remove them.**

There are two types of abbreviated word: the *abbreviation* (*UK*, *EU*, *CERN*); and the *contraction* (*Dr*, *Mr*, *incl* etc.). There are myriad approaches to punctuating these but they tend to come under two umbrella principles: keep the stops; and remove the stops. The British and American approaches differ markedly on the use of (.) marks. This tiny, round speck of ink is known generally as a *full stop* in British English, and *stop* or *full point* in the publishing trade. The standard name in the US is a *period*. (I will use *stop* for all from here onwards.)

The two main approaches governing stops are: the traditional style, favoured in the US, which uses stops with almost every abbreviation; and the modern style, favoured in the UK, which keeps stops to a minimum because it is felt that they often serve no real purpose in modern communications once they become household names.

| | |
|---|---|
| BBC | UK |
| NHS | MOT |
| HIV | IMF |

British writers would shudder at the thought of consistently writing *E.U.*, *U.K.* and *U.S.* – this just looks too stilted. Instead, the norm in British

English is *EU*, *UK* and *US*. (They also never write *U.S.A.* or *USA*, which is used only in American English.) It is also customary to remove stops after most abbreviations, such as *Inc*, *Ltd*, *Pty Ltd* and *Corp*. Americans, on the other hand, are horrified by the idea of this and they would quickly re-insert the periods to make *Inc.*, *Ltd.*, *Pty Ltd.* and *Corp.*

Americans not only have a fondness for including middle initials in people's names, they also like to always include stops after the initial. There is no need for the full stop after any initials in British English (this remains American practice).

| **BRITISH ENGLISH** | **AMERICAN ENGLISH** |
|---|---|
| ✓ John F Kennedy | ✓ John F. Kennedy |
| ✓ JK Rowling | ✓ J.K. Rowling |

Both traditional and modern approaches usually agree on the following:

**BRITISH ENGLISH**

| | |
|---|---|
| ✓ mph | ✓ Dr |
| ✓ Rt Hon. | ✓ Corp |
| ✓ Plc | ✓ Co |
| ✓ Inc | ✓ Pty Ltd |
| ✓ cf | ✓ St (Saint) |
| ✓ Jr | ✓ Sr |
| ✓ Mr | ✓ Rev. |
| ✓ a.m. | ✓ p.m. |
| ✓ No. 5 | ✓ i.e., |
| ✓ e.g., | ✓ Prof. |
| ✓ a.s.a.p | ✓ etc. |
| ✓ km/h | ✓ fig. |
| ✓ aka. | ✓ PhD |
| ✓ No. | ✓ Dr |
| ✓ Prof. | ✓ RSVP |
| ✓ AD | ✓ BC |
| ✓ vs | |

**AMERICAN ENGLISH**

| | |
|---|---|
| ✓ m.p.h. | ✓ Dr. |
| ✓ U.S./U.S.A | ✓ U.K. |
| ✓ Corp. | ✓ Co. |
| ✓ Inc. | ✓ Ltd. |
| ✓ cf. | ✓ St. (Saint) |
| ✓ Jr. | ✓ Sr. |
| ✓ Mr. | ✓ Rev. |
| ✓ a.m. | ✓ p.m. |

✓ No. 5          ✓ i.e.,
✓ e.g.,          ✓ Prof.
✓ a.s.a.p        ✓ etc.
✓ km/h           ✓ fig.
✓ a.k.a.         ✓ Ph.D
✓ Mrs.           ✓ Dr.
✓ Prof.          ✓ R.S.V.P.
✓ A.D.           ✓ B.C.
✓ vs.

On a final note, there is an increasing trend in the UK of capitalising only the first letter of longer acronyms, such as *Nato* instead of *NATO*, *Nasa* instead of *NASA*, *Uefa* instead of *UEFA* and *Cern* instead of *CERN*. The supposed justification for this is that these words are pronounced as words rather than letters (not "C-I-A" for example) but this system is not recommended, even if this is what has happened to radar (formerly R.A.D.A.R) and scuba (S.C.U.B.A). Instead, all-caps are to be preferred.

**✓ I have heard of UEFA, NASA and NATO, but not CERN.**
✗ *I have heard of Uefa, Nasa and Nato, but not Cern.*

# 36

## euros

### *What's the capital of euro?*

✓ **We accept dollars, pesos, pounds and euros.**
✗ *We accept Dollars, Pesos, Pounds and Euros.*
✓ **1 euro and 25 euros**
✗ *1 euro and 25 euro*

✓ **€100**
✗ *100€*
✗ *E100*

**Write *1 euro*, *25 euros* and *€100*, always remembering to use a lowercase e in *euro*.**

Since its inception in 1999, many people are still confused about *euros*, especially English speakers.

It is obvious why people often confuse *euros* (with a small *e*) and *Europe*, *European* etc. (with an uppercase *e*) but it doesn't make *Euro* correct. Treat *euros* just as you would other currencies such as *dollars*, *pesos* or *pounds*. Do not write *Euros* unless it is at the start of a sentence.

✓ **I managed to spend a hundred euros on lunch and a taxi.**
✗ *I managed to spend a hundred Euros on lunch and a taxi.*

As computers played catch-up to include the € symbol onto keyboards, many (especially British) publishers defaulted to a capital E as a substitute because they either couldn't produce one or for fear that it would not reproduce properly when printed or on screen. The € symbol is now established enough that this practice can no longer be justified. Every writer should take a few moments to find out which combination of keys on your keyboard gives you €. (In the case of a Mac, it is alt + 2.)

Many countries in continental Europe employ the euro symbol after the number in their own language, such as *50€*. However, this should not be done when writing in English. Instead, stick to *€50* and *50 euros*.

The correct plural form of *euro* is *euros*, not *euro*. Ignore any suggestion that this is not so, including from your word processor. It is possible that your software will try to convince you to change *20 euros* into *20 Euros*, *20 euro* or – heaven forbid – *20 euro's*. Ignore it.

Last, this same principle applies to *eurozone*, the group of countries that use the euro – again, not to be used with a capital E.

> ✓ **Denmark, Sweden and the UK remain outside the eurozone.**
> ✗ *Denmark, Sweden and the UK remain outside the Eurozone.*

# 37

## stray capitals

*Stray capitals make Troublesome Weeding*

✓ **I married a doctor.**
✗ *I married a Doctor.*
✓ **I have been in Finland in spring and summer but never in winter.**
✗ *I have been in Finland in Spring and Summer but never in Winter.*
✓ **There is only one way out of this crisis: a radical redistribution of resources.**
✗ *There is only one way out of this crisis: A radical redistribution of resources.*

**Review your writing and be on the lookout for stray words that are capitalised for no reason. Capital letters are spreading faster than the plague these days.**

Capital letters are like Weeds. No matter how much You trim them back, more Capital letters keep appearing. Inserting Weird and wonderful Capitals at Random is becoming increasingly common these Days and it seems as though many Writers have Forgotten how to use Them.

✗ *Our Bank Managers are here to help.*
✗ *I love to watch Reality TV.*
✗ *You must sign up for our Mobile Banking service.*

There is no need to capitalise *bank manager*, which gets treated the same as if it were *employees*, *flight attendant*, *pilot* etc. Equally, *reality TV* does not need a capital R. That is because they are just normal words. The typical mistake is to think that job or occupation is a job title. And mobile banking, well, there is no need for Caps – I mean, caps.

✓ **Our employees/pilots/flight attendants are here to help.**
✗ *Our Employees/Pilots/Flight Attendants are here to help.*
✓ **We value our customers.**
✗ *We value our Customers.*
✓ **We only drink champagne that is from Champagne.**
✗ *We only drink Champagne that is from champagne.*

This might seem like common sense, but stray capitals are cropping up at an alarming rate of knots. This is especially true of advertising and a lot of corporate materials. Not only are new products being given names with weird combinations of upper- and lower-case letters, there is a lot of random capitals in general. This advertisement appeared in the press at the time of writing:

> ✘ *Double Discounts plus Extra Savings ends Monday. Plus there's Free Credit on Every Bed.*

This is pointless capitalisation, and not proper English. Here, the writer is presumably trying to accentuate the force of the *discounts*, *savings*, *credit* and *beds* on offer. But capitals should not be used in this way. If, however, "Every Bed" were a trademarked name, then capital letters would be justified – although I suspect that this is not the case.

Some common mistakes using capitals include the following:

**THE FOUR SEASONS**
✓ **winter, spring, summer and autumn/fall**
✘ *Winter, Spring, Summer and Autumn/Fall*

**AWARDS AND PRIZES**
✓ **the Booker prize, a Grammy award and Nobel prize**
✘ *the Booker Prize, a Grammy Award and Nobel Prize*

**JOB DESCRIPTIONS**
✓ **I married a lawyer.**
✘ *I married a Lawyer.*
✓ **We need to recruit a new manager.**
✘ *We need to recruit a new Manager.*

**OUTER SPACE**
✓ **We can see the whole universe. It is as hot as the Sun.**
✘ *We can see the whole Universe. It is as hot as the sun.*

**-ISMS**
✓ **cubism, dadaism, nazism, modernism, communism**
✘ *Cubism, Dadaism, Nazism, Modernism, Communism*

You can be forgiven for thinking that the -isms above might have needed capitals, but standard practice in fact is not to do so. However, why people insist on putting a capital p in *Nobel prize* and more than one capital a in

*Academy award*, a capital u in *universe* and a capital w in plain old *winter*, I don't know. But it happens all the time. Don't be one of them. These would only have capitals when they start a line or sentence.

By contrast, *do* use capitals with the following:

## TRADEMARKS
✓ **Apple, the Royal Bank of Scotland, Big Macs, the New York Times**
✗ *apple, the royal bank of Scotland, big macs, the new york times*

## PROPER NAMES
✓ **the Home Office, Christmas Day, the Bar, the Queen's speech, the Pope, the Queen, the Prime Minister, the House of Lords, a Caesarian, the Official Secrets Act**
✗ *the home office, christmas day, the bar, the queen's speech, the pope, the queen, the prime minister, the house of lords, a caesarcan, the official secrets act*

## TITLES
✓ **I married a doctor.**
✗ *I married a Doctor.*
✓ **I am here to see the doctor.**
✗ *I am here to see the Doctor.*
✓ **I have an appointment with Doctor Davidson.**
✗ *I have an appointment with doctor Davidson.*
✓ **This is the new head of marketing.**
✗ *This is the new Head of Marketing.*

*Doctor* is both a normal word and a title. Only use a capital when using titles, not when describing occupations.

## NAMES OF REGIONS
✓ **eastern Europe, southern hemisphere, the West of England**
✗ *Eastern Europe, Southern Hemisphere, the west of England*

## RELIGIONS, ORDERS, PARTIES, MOVEMENTS
✓ **Christians, Masons, Tories, Feminism, Labour, Lib Dems**
✗ *christians, masons, tories, feminism, labour, lib dems*

## DAYS OF THE WEEK, MONTHS
✓ **Monday, June**
✗ *monday, june*

Finally, a few more examples of where not to use capitals:

### FOR EMPHASIS
✓ **50% off all furniture, rugs and curtains**
✗ *50% off all Furniture, Rugs & Curtains*
✓ **Great prices on all technology**
✗ *Great prices on ALL Technology*

### JOB DESCRIPTIONS
✓ **Do you have sales experience?**
✗ *Do you have Sales experience?*
✓ **Have you met our new financial auditor?**
✗ *Have you met our new Financial Auditor?*

Last of all, there is a lot of confusion about capitals with headlines and after colons, a lot of which can be confused with American practices.

It is standard practice in the UK to treat a headline as a normal sentence as far as capitals go. In the US, however, it is standard practice to capitalise every initial letter in a sentence, using so-called sentence case.

### HEADLINES
✓ **(UK) Online companies fight endless war against computer attacks.**
✗ *(UK) Online Companies Fight Endless War Against Computer Attacks.*
✓ **(US) Online Companies Fight Endless War Against Computer Attacks.**

Similarly, it is standard practice in American English to use an initial capital after a colon, but not in British English:

### COLONS (UK)
✓ **When Shakespeare met Seuss: mashing up literature.**
✓ **It all comes down to this: think positive and say 'Yes' to everything.**
✓ **There is only one way out of this crisis: hard work.**

### COLONS (US)
✓ **When Shakespeare Met Seuss: Mashing Up Literature.**
✓ **It all comes down to this: Think positive and say 'Yes' to everything.**
✓ **There is only one way out of this crisis: Hard work.**

There is no need for capitals after the colon in British English, whether it is a title of a book or a normal two-part sentence.

# 38

## further versus farther
### *There is no need for farther discussion*

✓ **You must try to make your money go further.**
✗ *You must try to make your money go farther.*
✓ **How much further do we have to walk?**
✗ *How much farther do we have to walk?*
✓ **This building is closed until further notice.**
✗ *This building is closed until farther notice.*
✓ **I see this as a chance to further my career.**
✗ *I see this as a chance to farther my career.*

**It is complete nonsense that** *farther* **and** *further* **apply differently to aspects of time and space. Both mean the same thing and** *further* **is the standard spelling in both Britain and the US.**

*Further* is the original spelling from Old English and *farther* is nothing more than a variant spelling. You may have heard that *farther* and *further* each occupies different linguistic territory; that *farther* relates only to physical location or distance because it comes from far. It does not. This idea is pure folk etymology, i.e. nonsense.

While only *further* can mean, "moreover", "extra", "additional", (*farther* does not), both *farther* and *further* are used for the concept of distance. Although *farther* remains a legitimate variant spelling – and nothing more – it has no exclusive ownership or monopoly rights to the meaning "distance". *Further* is the standard spelling and the one to be preferred in every circumstance where the paths of these two words cross. The best approach is to consign *farther* to the trash, I mean, the rubbish bin.

✓ **I don't think I can walk any further.**
✗ *I don't think I can walk any farther.*

The "farther = distance only" myth is more prevalent in the US than it is in Britain – though it is creeping in. The *Times* newspaper uses it a lot,

93

for some strange reason. There was a period in the early 1900s when the concept was toyed with in Britain but it never really took hold. The overall prevalence of *farther* in the UK is low and sometimes based on the equally wrong assumption that it is also a literary or formal variant. Again, it is not. None of these claims are true. *Farther* and *farthest* are best dropped from your vocabulary altogether.

For those who are interested in the etymology, *further* comes from Old English *furþur* (þ became *th*), which was the comparative form of *forth*; *farther* later began as a variant spelling of *further* and came alongside the newly coined *farrer* and *ferrer* comparatives for *far* in the 1100s; it was *further* (and *farther*) that together muscled in on the territory of comparatives for *far* (from their original territory *forth*), *farrer* and *ferrer*. *Further* and *farther* ultimately consigned them to dialect status by the 1600s (Shakespeare preferred *further* over *farther* 80% of the time in his writing). It was not until the late 1800s that attempts were made to link *farther* to mean, "farrer" only and deny *further* the same privilege. Why don't we just reinstate *farrer*?

# 39

## quote, unquote

*"You can even quote me on it."*

✓ **What did the 0 say to the 8? "Nice belt."**
✗ *What did the 0 say to the 8? "Nice belt".*
✓ **The clergyman said, "You may kiss the bride".**
✓ **The clergyman said: "You may kiss the bride."**

✓ **"These findings do not answer all of our questions," she replied, "but most questions related to this field cannot be answered without them."**

**Getting punctuation right when using *quotation marks* is less difficult than people assume. The first thing to get right is whether or not to use single or double quotes. The second thing then is to work out whether the commas and full stops go inside or outside the quotes. (Note: American English operates differently in that the stop (period) always goes inside the quotes no matter whether it is a partial or a full quote.)**

### SINGLE OR DOUBLE QUOTES?

It is best to stick with double quotes as your default style. This is not the only way, but it the most common system in newspapers, magazines and journalism. Book publishers follow the same rules that I am about to explain, but usually with the roles of single/double quotes reversed. Some publications follow the mantra, "single quotes for the written and double quotes for the spoken, and single quotes for quotes within quotes".

#### STOPS: INSIDE OR OUT?
✓ **The fireman said, "There is no smoke without fire".**

Note the capital letter starting the quote as well as the stop being outside the quotation marks. It could also use a colon (:) instead of the comma.

This would also have a capital letter and the full stop inside the quotation marks.

> ✓ **The fireman said: "There is no smoke without fire."**

The first point, then, is to point out that quotes come in various lengths: one word, several individual words, a string of words, a complete sentence and more than one sentence. The purpose of quotation marks and punctuation is to separate your own words from the words of others.

> ✓ **The Home Office has said it is now a "priority" to investigate.**

Here, the writer has inserted single words into his text, using double quotes to illustrate that *priority* and *awful* are not his or her opinions. This same principle works with several words quoted separately. When the quote appears at the end of the sentence, the *full stop* stays outside it because it ends the sentence – not the quote.

> ✓ **They all said that the film was "awful".**
> ✗ *They all said that the film was "awful."*
> ✓ **Mr Nash, 45, said he was "surprised" and "frightened" when the "very hostile" man ran up to him on a South London street.**

Another common mistake is to include a full stop after a question mark or exclamation mark.

> ✓ **He asked me: "What is the nature of consciousness?"**
> ✗ *He asked me: "What is the nature of consciousness?".*
> ✗ *He asked me: "What is the nature of consciousness?."*

## COMMAS

Next, commas can either go inside or outside the quotes, depending on the context.

> ✓ **The book has been described as "a work of genius", "a marvel" and "unput-downable".**
> ✗ *The book has been described as "a work of genius," "a marvel" and "unput-downable."*

Again, the stop here ends the sentence and not the quotes. The comma stays outside because it does not belongs to the quote and serves to separate the first two quotes from the third as a list. The same is true when the quote falls at the end of a middle clause:

> ✓ **Mr Nash gave a long presentation, entitled "Berlin", to 1000 industry delegates.**
> ✗ *Mr Nash gave a presentation, entitled "Berlin," to 1000 industry delegates.*

Once again, the *comma* remains outside the quote marks. However, there is one situation where the full stop falls inside the end quote:

> ✓ **Environmental campaigners remain sceptical about the company's sincerity, but a spokesperson reiterate that it "is committed to sustainability and maintains high standards. This is evident in the latest £4 million investment programme last year."**

Here, because the quote is partial yet goes over more than one sentence, the usual *full stop* outside now goes inside the quotation marks to end both the sentence and the quote.

You will no doubt have seen commas inside quotes and may now be wondering where you have seen them used. The answer: when sentences begin with a quote.

> ✓ **"I don't feel well," said Mr Nash.**
> ✗ *"I don't feel well", said Mr Nash.*

This time, the comma goes inside to indicate the rest of the sentence. If the quote continues, then the next quote appears as a complete sentence, including the full stop, inside quotes.

> ✓ **"I am trying to track down a lost parcel," said Mr Nash, who was losing his patience. "I know that it should have arrived at the depot by now."**
> ✗ *"I am trying to track down a lost parcel", said Mr Nash, who was losing his patience. "I know that it should have arrived at the depot by now".*

## COLON OR COMMA?

This is typical presentation for reported speech: to begin a sentence with a quote, introduce the speaker and continue with the next quote.

✓ "We are positive about the future," said Monica Ålgars, spokesperson for the company. "Orders have picked up significantly in the last month."

✗ *"We are positive about the future", said Monica Ålgars, spokesperson for the company, "orders have picked up significantly in the last month."*

Another way of doing the same thing is:

✓ Mr Nash said: "I am trying to track down a lost parcel. I know that it should have arrived at the depot by now."

✗ *Mr Nash said, "I am trying to track down a lost parcel. I know that it should have arrived at the depot by now."*

By starting with the speaker and cutting straight to the quote, both of these methods achieve the same thing. The difference is merely stylistic. The *colon style* is preferred in journalism and the *comma style* is more common in books, especially with dialogue. This is a useful way to write out quotes that are complete sentences, and the full stop remains inside because it ends the quote (and, by default, the sentence).

One thing that is unique to journalism is what happens when extended quotes go on for several sentences.

✓ "I was there when it happened," said Danny, 24, from Colchester. "I saw the whole thing.

[new paragraph]

✓ "This woman came in and started shouting and ranting at the other customers in the queue.

[new paragraph]

✓ "The security guard came over to speak to her and kindly asked her to be calm or leave.

[new paragraph]

✓ "That's when she became irate and began pulling items off shelves and throwing them."

Notice three things: from the first line onwards there is *no closing quote* after the full stop; and that the close quote appears only at the end of the last sentence; and that the witness, Danny, does not need to be mentioned more than once even though his quotes continue for three more paragraphs.

This is normal in newspapers where, because they use narrow columns, tend to make each paragraph a complete sentence. In a magazine or online story the four lines could be made into one paragraph, starting with opening quotes as:

> ✓ **"I was there when it happened," said Danny, 24, from Colchester. "I saw…and throwing them."**

## QUOTES WITHIN QUOTES

For *quotes within quotes*, the inner quote is set between single quotes (often the other way round in book publishing). Over two paragraphs this would look like this:

> ✓ **The witness said: "The gunman told me, 'Hand over your money', in a loud, aggressive way.**
> ✓ **"He then shouted at us and said, 'Do it now or I will shoot'."**
> ✗ *The witness said: "The gunman told me, "Hand over your money," in a loud, aggressive way.*
> ✗ *"He then shouted at us and said, "Do it now or I will shoot.""*

The things to notice here are: the comma stays outside the inner quote in the first sentence; and when it ends the sentence the full stop stays within both quotes, not between.

# 40

## the serial comma

*What is red, white and blue with no comma?*

✓ (UK) I am going for a drink with Paul, Charlotte and Helen.
✗ *(UK) I am going for a drink with Paul, Charlotte, and Helen.*
✓ (US) I am going for a drink with Paul, Charlotte, and Helen.

**There is no need for a comma before *and* in a list of three or more things using British English. In American English, however, a comma is required before *and*. (It is also known as a serial comma or "Oxford comma" when used in British English. This should be used only for stylistic reasons – if at all – or to add clarity in complicated lists.)**

First, there is a lot of confusion about whether or not there should be a *comma after and in a list*. In standard British no such comma is needed.

**STANDARD BRITISH, CANADIAN AND AUSTRALIAN ENGLISH**
✓ Red, white and blue
✓ Eat, drink and be merry.

Extra commas do crop up in writing, however, but mostly because American English always requires one and because a minority of publishers in the UK chooses to follow this same method. The publishers of the *Oxford English Dictionary*, Oxford University Press, do just this, which is how the "Oxford comma" got its name. However, this practice goes against the grain of standard British English.

**STANDARD AMERICAN ENGLISH**
✓ Red, white, and blue
✓ Eat, drink, and be merry.

**NON-STANDARD BRITISH ENGLISH ("OXFORD COMMA")**
✓ Red, white, and blue
✓ Eat, drink, and be merry.

Second, a more common problem area involves what I will call "list commas" – these should be used between strings of descriptive words (adjectives) to describe another.

✓ **I saw a fluffy, black cat.**
✗ *I saw a fluffy black cat.*

Each attribute must be separated by a comma when more than one word is used to describe something, such as fluffy and black.

✓ **I took a photo of the happy, blushing bride.**
✗ *I took a photo of the happy blushing bride.*
✓ **Women like tall, dark and handsome men.**
✗ *Women like tall dark and handsome men.*

Advertisers are frequent abusers of forgetting to use list commas. They love to inject their copy with adjectives – and it is almost impossible to write more than a few lines of advertising copy without them – but the men and women of ad land often go overboard. Their message becomes hard to read when they omit commas from the right places.

Move over to brand new low start fixed rate deal

Third, the next level up from using list commas correctly is to remember to use hyphens if *compounds* are used (see **31**, **44**, **52**, **53**, **63**, **81** and **90**):

✓ **Instant, full-body volume mascara**
✗ *Instant full body volume mascara*
✓ **A fresh, olive-blossom fragrance**
✗ *A fresh olive blossom fragrance*
✓ **Lip-contour, smoothing cream**
✗ *Lip contour smoothing cream*
✓ **Easy-cook, long-grain rice**
✗ *Easy cook long grain rice*
✓ **High-impact-curling mascara**
✗ *High impact curling mascara*
✓ **Available as white, grey, peacock and pink, cultured, freshwater pearls**
✗ *Available as white grey peacock and pink cultured freshwater pearls*

As you can see, not having commas to separate each attribute correctly can make it difficult to read.

# 41

## that versus who and whose
### *Don't you know that I am?*

✓ **I have a friend who had the exact same problem last week.**
✗ *I have a friend that had the exact same problem last week.*

**Use *who* instead of *that* when referring to people, and *that* for things, organisations and groups of people.**

It is common in spoken English to say *that* instead of *who*, and sometimes the other way round. Few will worry about this but it is more important to get it right in formal contexts and in print.

✓ **Sir Donald Bradman was the greatest cricketer who ever lived.**
✗ *Sir Donald Bradman was the greatest cricketer that ever lived.*
✓ **I would rather buy goods from a company that cares about the environment.**
✗ *I would rather buy goods from a company who cares about the environment.*
✓ **He was the one who did it.**
✗ *He was the one that did it.*

When *groups* of people have a particular name (*team*, *squad*, *troupe*, *gang*, *congregation*), treat them as inanimate things by using *that* instead of *who*. Do not use *that* for types of people (*troops*, *nurses*, *friends* etc.).

✓ **Police are searching for a gang of four that robbed the jewellery store this morning.**
✗ *Police are searching for a gang of four who robbed the jewellery store this morning.*
✓ **This new tax measure rewards families that don't save.**
✗ *This new tax measure rewards families who don't save.*
✓ **The Prime Minister paid tribute to the troops who had served in the Vietnam War.**
✗ *The Prime Minister paid tribute to the troops that had served in the Vietnam War.*

This same principle applies to any reference to a *representative* of a group (*Christians*, *singles*, *retirees* etc.) or a type of person (*Goth*, *surfer* etc.).

> ✓ **This new dating service is designed for the single man that is looking for love.**
> ✗ *This new dating service is designed for the single man who is looking for love.*
> ✓ **Any person that thinks like that deserves to be told off.**
> ✗ *Any person who thinks like that deserves to be told off.*

Animals do not count as humans. No matter how much they are part of the family, they must be used with *that*.

> ✓ **Did you hear about the dog that kept stealing food from the convenience store?**
> ✗ *Did you hear about the dog who kept stealing food from the convenience store?*

It is, however, perfectly correct to use *whose* with inanimate (non-human) things. While there may have been grumbles about this in the past, it is accepted as correct because it avoids the awkward inclusion of *of which* or *of whose*.

> ✓ **the mountain whose trees...**
> ✗ *the mountain, the trees of which...*
> ✓ **the building whose façade...**
> ✗ *the building, of whose façade...*

In situations where it is not clear between *who* and *that*, use *that*. (For the difference between *that* and *which*, see **30**.)

# 42

## fill in a form and tick a box
### *Check this out!*

✓ (UK) **Please fill in this form and return it.**
✓ (US) **Please fill out this form and return it.**
✓ (UK) **Can you fill in the rest of your details, please?**
✓ (US) **Can you fill out the rest of your details, please?**

**In British English you** *fill in a form* **and you** *tick a box*. **In American English you** *fill out a form* **and** *check a box*.

In British English *fill in* means "insert" or "complete" information that is missing and *fill out* means "add bulk" or "padding".

✗ *(UK) We need to fill out the rest of the form.*
✓ **You have filled out significantly since your teens.**
✓ **My essay is pretty much written but I need to fill it out with a few more paragraphs.**

Similarly, filling in the small boxes on a questionnaire or multiple-choice exam is to *tick a box* (with a tick ✓) in British English not *check* one. In American English the expression is *check a box* (with a cross ✗). *Check* in British English has the meaning "to inspect", so *check the box* means, "inspect the box", not mark it in any way.

✓ **This report needs filling out, it is too brief.**
✗ *This report needs filling in, it is too brief.*
✓ (UK) **Please tick the box if you wish to be anonymous.**
✓ (US) **Please check the box if you wish to be anonymous.**

The dominance of American English means that *fill out* is slowly creeping into British English, so it is worth keeping a keen eye out for and avoiding this American contender.

# 43

## -ly + hyphen
### *Strictly no hyphen needed*

✓ **Freshly squeezed orange juice.**
✗ *Freshly-squeezed orange juice.*
✓ **A badly executed plan.**
✗ *A badly-executed plan.*
✓ **A strictly enforced rule.**
✗ *A strictly-enforced rule.*

## Remove any *hyphens* falling immediately after any *-ly* adverbs.

This is a common but understandable mistake. Those who understand the difference between a *small business plan* and *a small-business plan* (see **90**) might be tempted to write *a badly-designed building* because it follows the same logic. Unfortunately, it doesn't.

✓ **A neatly written letter.**
✗ *A neatly-written letter.*
✓ **A badly needed holiday.**
✗ *A badly-needed holiday.*

The *-ly* suffix denotes an *adverb*. Adverbs don't get hyphenated. Stick to *freshly squeezed OJ*, *neatly written letter* and *badly needed holiday*.

✗ *highly-skilled workers*
✗ *wrongly-convicted man*
✗ *frequently-asked questions*
✗ *bitterly-disappointing result*

Note, however, that not all -ly words are adverbs. *Early* is not always an adverb:

✓ **I always start the working week with an early-morning run.**
✗ *I always start the working week with an early morning run.*
✓ **We want to target early-career scientists and early-years teachers.**

✓ **They are building a new early-warning system.**

The *early* here is an adjective (it describes nouns/things, not verbs/ actions). That is why it needs a hyphen. (See also **31**, **44**, **52**, **53**, **63**, **81** and **90**.)

# 44

## hyphen (-) versus en rule (–)
### *Always remember the golden en rules*

✓ **Tell me – when you can – if you are coming.**
✗ *Tell me - when you can - if you are coming.*
✓ **2009–2010 Senior product manager, JK Books, London**
✗ *2009-2010 Senior product manager, JK Books, London*
✓ **16–19-year-old students**
✗ *16-19-year-old students*
✓ **Mon–Fri 9–5**
✗ *Mon-Fri 9-5*

**The *en rule* is a hallmark of professional writing, and professional writers need to know the difference between using "-", "–" and "—". The term *en rule* is used in the UK and Australia. It is known as an *en dash* in the US and Canada, and in computing code.**

First, the *hyphen* (-) is the short one; used to join compound words (see **81** and **90**) and prefixes (*co-own*, *anti-Semitic*). The *en rule* (–) is the longer one that draws relationships between items by linking them together (*US–UK relations*, *in the 18–30 age group*, *10–20 kg*). When used in this way, there are no spaces on either side of the en rule.

The en rule gets its name from equalling the width of the *letter n*. (There is also such a thing as an *em rule* (—), which is the width of an *m*. This book does not cover it because they are not standard in British English and are more commonly used in the US. However, there are exceptions. The *Economist*, for example, uses the in the closed-up style—like this.)

✓ **We need models aged 16–23.**
✗ *We need models aged 16-23*
✓ **Franco–American relations**
✗ *Franco-American relations*

Second, the en rule is also used in pairs to cut sharp *digressions* into sentences; a change in tack that is more severe – such as this – than using commas to insert an extra clause. When used in a sentence this way it traditionally includes spaces on either side. (Some publishers, and often in the US, close up the gap even here, as well as singularly and serving the role of a colon – like this.)

The mistake to avoid – especially in professional writing – is to use a hyphen (-) where an en rule (–) is required.

> ✓ **She loves Italian fashion – Gucci is her favourite label – and she hopes ultimately to work in the industry.**
> ✗ *She loves Italian fashion - Gucci is her favourite label - and she hopes ultimately to work in the industry.*
> ✓ **Two Commonwealth countries – Australia and Canada – want to host the next Olympic games.**
> ✗ *Two Commonwealth countries - Australia and Canada - want to host the next Olympic games.*

> ✓ **2010–2011 Purchasing manager for a large company in...**
> ✗ *2010-2011 Purchasing manager for a large company in...*

> ✓ **The target audience is A, B, C females aged 16–23.**
> ✗ *The target audience is A, B, C females aged 16-23.*
> ✓ **add 5–50g of butter.**
> ✗ *add 5 – 50g of butter.*

All of the above examples need (–) instead of (-). It is not an unforgivable sin to use the hyphen in personal writing and correspondence, but it is a standard that is firmly adhered to by professional writers. What you don't want is for a bunch of short lines (-) on the printed page.

This misuse of the hyphen is also prevalent on the web, perhaps by people who don't know HTML code. To make it an en rule on-screen, use the code *&ndash;*. American writers sometimes use -- in place of –, but this is not standard in British English.

Third, the en rule is used with *spaces either side* when used with a range using mixed units:

> ✓ **I have several parcels weighing 500g – 1.5kg.**
> ✗ *I have several parcels weighing 500g–1.5kg.*
> ✓ **Open 29 May – 1 June.**
> ✗ *Open 29 May–1 June.*

The last point is this: to overuse the en rule is to misuse it. These should be used sparingly. Like commas, too many can begin to cause confusion.

# 45

## don't use double double spaces
### *Are you seeing double?*

✓ **The letter arrived yesterday. It had been opened.**
✗ *The letter arrived yesterday.  It had been opened.*

**It is no longer necessary to have *two spaces after a full stop* to start a new sentence.··Like this.··This practice came and went with the typewriter.··They are not always easy to spot but a Find/Replace search is always a good way to avoid them.**

The idea that there needed to be *double spaces* (not to be confused with double spacing, which is the gap between the lines of text on a page) after a full stop came and went with the era of the typewriter. This was because they often used so-called monospaced typefaces – letters of equal width and spacing – and two spaces were believed to be clearer and easier to read than single spaces. By this, I mean the once-common practice of ending every sentence with a tap, tap of the spacebar after every full stop. [tap] [tap] The (false) idea that double spaces are correct still exists among some writers, especially in the US. [tap][tap] They are, however, no longer required.

It is a long time since even the dotcom bubble and bust. Computers are everywhere and this holdover from the days of the typewriter should be weeded out of all professional writing. The only thing that they do is create more work in having to remove them at a later stage. When double spaces are missed in proofing they can add weird and unsightly gaps. Like this.  And this.

# 46

## You and I... (we)
### *If I were you, we would be*

✓ **You and I (we) should have a drink together.**
✗ *You and me should have a drink together.*

**Put simply, *you and I* means, "we". It is a myth that *you and I* is always correct no matter what. Use it towards the beginning of a sentence (see 47) when "we" is the grammatical subject.**

we = you and I

While the rule above is a simplistic and overly general one, it works re-markably well whenever you are in any doubt about which is correct. If you can replace your construction with *we* (instead of *us*), and it sounds correct, then it should be the right choice.

There is often confusion whether it is *you and me* or *you and I*. Again, swapping *us/we* quickly sorts out right from wrong on this matter.

There was a time when *You and I* was forcefully considered correct even as the grammatical object, but this is no longer so. Between *you and me* (us), anything else is just wrong. (See also **47**.)

# 47

## ...you and me (us)

### *If you were me and we were us*

✓ **Nobody, not even me, knows the answer to this problem.**
✗ *Nobody, not even I, knows the answer to this problem.*
✓ **This letter is addressed to you and me (us).**
✗ *This letter is addressed to you and I.*

*You and me* **means, "*us*". Use it in the middle or end of a sentence.**

us = you and me

Put simply, *you and me* means, "us". It is a myth that *you and I* is always correct in all cases. Use it towards the end of a sentence (see **46**) when you would normally use *us*.

While the above is a simplistic, general rule, it is a good one to remember for times when you are in doubt. If you can replace your construction with *us* (instead of *we*), and it sounds correct, then it will be the right choice.

# 48

## repetition
### *Did I mention that already?*

**Keep an eye out for *repeating words* in your writing and avoid repeating stock phrases in your writing.**

Did you notice the double use of repeated words in the sentence above? Chances are you did notice the repetition. Nothing is more tedious than someone repetitiously repeating words that they repeat over and over. Stripping out repetition is an aspect of writing that is important because, not only is repetition monotonous, but it is repetitious.

*Repetition* is easy to do and is something that we can all be guilty of. However, not everyone is aware of how often or when they do it, because it is not always easy to spot. The paragraph above used the obvious example of the derivative of *repeat* no fewer than eight times, which may be noticeable, but try this one:

> The real boom in processed and ready-made foods started in the 1960s, when increasing numbers of people started to move from the country to the cities.

Did you spot the repetition? One of the instances of *started* could be replaced with *began*. Some might argue that going to such trouble is unnecessary, but these two words appeared in a single sentence. How many times would be acceptable to use *repeat* over a one-hour presentation? How soon before you started to sound like a politician or salesman instead of a speaker? Business people and politicians fast become tiresome to listen to because they repeat themselves over and over: "...*going forward...going forward...going forward...going forward...*" Zzzzzz.

One aspect of good communication is being aware of your own repetition and stock phrases. Rather than reinforcing the importance of your words, you run the risk of diluting your message.

Another common type of *repetition* is the practice of not varying the way a person is referred to in an article. Instead of referring to *Mr Cameron* or

112

*Cameron* over and over again, try writing *he, the Prime Minister, the PM, the Tory leader, the popular/unpopular leader, the self-proclaimed family man* etc. This will give your writing more depth and prevent monotony.

# 49

## man/woman versus chair
### *For every man, woman and chair*

**Using *non-sexist words* is less about "correctness", "censorship" or avoiding "offence" than it is about ensuring neutrality.**

Some people object to tampering with language for political purposes. Others simply hate being told what they should and shouldn't do. The typical response will be to label something as "political correctness". Whether language determines the world or merely influences it is not the point of choosing gender-neutral words: the point is fairness and the aim is courtesy.

Unlike Finnish, which has one word for he/she, *hän*, English lacks a gender-free, singular form of *they*, *their*, *theirs* or *them*. Instead we have to use *he*, *him*, *his*, *she*, *hers* and *her*. There is no gender-neutral way of referring to someone in the third person. English does, however, have a long tradition of gender-specific vocabulary relating to titles, occupations and working life. In a world where women and men both work to support their families, certain categories of words have become outmoded.

The word that is most commonly scrutinised in the corporate world is *chairman*. The neutral term for this is now *chair* or *chairperson*. Another common example is *spokesman*, now *spokesperson*.

> ✓ **Helen Davidson will take over as chair in the spring.**
> ✗ *Helen Davidson will take over as chairman in the spring.*

Now, while some see it fitting to use female equivalents, such as *spokeswoman* and *chairwoman*, these are not to be recommended because these go against the principle of fostering neutrality. Expressions like this are more likely to stand out and highlight for no good reason that someone is a woman.

Bear in mind that there is debate about these terms. Some people do find *-person* suffixes unsatisfactory, "messing with language" or "verbal pollutants", while others regard *chair* on its own as ridiculous. Some claim that men are being excluded from discourse, if *chair* is used, but others argue that a *spokeswoman* by definition cannot speak for men's views. Maybe *speaker*, like *chair*, is better? Who knows?

But this is all a distraction from the central purpose of what is being aimed for: neutrality and common courtesy. Today, everyone is an *actor, millionaire, waiter, conductor* etc.

There is a whole host of words, titles and occupations using the suffix *-man* that have changed over the past decades:

| | |
|---|---|
| ✓ **camera operator** | ✓ **supervisor** |
| ✗ *cameraman* | ✗ *foreman* |
| ✓ **police officer** | ✓ **postal worker** |
| ✗ *policeman* | ✗ *postman* |
| ✓ **working hours** | ✓ **humankind** |
| ✗ *man-hours* | ✗ *mankind* |
| ✓ **staffing** | ✓ **workforce** |
| ✗ *manning* | ✗ *manpower* |
| ✓ **artificial** | ✓ **repairer** |
| ✗ *man-made* | ✗ *repairman, handyman* |
| ✓ **bartender** | ✓ **sales assistant /salesperson** |
| ✗ *barman/barmaid* | ✗ *salesman/saleswoman* |
| ✓ **worker/road worker** | ✓ **member of the clergy** |
| ✗ *workman* | ✗ *clergyman/clergywoman* |
| ✓ **craftsperson** | ✓ **hero** |
| ✗ *craftsman* | ✗ *heroine* |
| ✓ **lay person** | ✓ **sports person** |
| ✗ *layman/laywoman* | ✗ *sportsman/sportswoman* |
| ✓ **leader, public figure** | ✓ **usher** |
| ✗ *statesman* | ✗ *usherette* |
| ✓ **flight attendant** | ✓ **meteorologist** |
| ✗ *steward/stewardess* | ✗ *weather man/weather girl* |

The only exceptions are *businessman* and *businesswoman*, for which no satisfactory equivalents exist. (Not everyone agrees that *businessperson* does the job.)

The next class of words are those using *-ess*. While many of these have been abolished, it is interesting to note that we haven't yet deemed it fit to change *goddess, baroness* and *princess*:

| | |
|---|---|
| ✓ **actor** | ✓ **manager** |
| ✗ *actress* | ✗ *manageress* |
| ✓ **millionaire** | ✓ **benefactor** |
| ✓ **millionairess** | ✓ **benefactress** |

✓ **waiter/waiting staff**
✗ *waitress*
✓ **author**
✗ *authoress*
✓ **head teacher**
✗ *headmistress*

✓ **seducer**
✗ *temptress*
✓ **sculptor**
✗ *sculptress*

Third, consider carefully whether gender needs to be assigned at all before writing something like *female doctor* – or worse, *lady doctor*. Does it matter that the doctor is female? Sometimes the context will make it necessary. But if this is not the case then *female* is redundant and only *doctor* is necessary.

✓ **I have a great doctor.**
✗ *I have a great female doctor.*
✓ **The train driver managed to avert disaster.**
✗ *The female train driver managed to avert disaster.*
✓ **A new wave of female firebrands is entering politics.**
✓ **Where are the female CEOs?**
✓ **Female gondolier ends 900 years of Venetian narrow-mindedness.**

Before you object to *midwife*, the word actually comes from Old English, meaning "with the woman".

# 50

## co-operate
### *Why not coop them apart?*

✓ **Co-operation**
✗ *Cooperation*
✓ **Co-producer**
✗ *Coproducer*

✓ **Co-ordinate**
✗ *Coordinate*
✓ **Co-worker**
✗ *coworker*

**There remains a strong tradition in British English to prefer *co-operate* etc. over *cooperate*, which is the preferred choice in American English.**

The world of prefixes is a murky one because there is always doubt about whether or not to hyphenate *re-*, *ex-*, *non-* and *sub-* etc. Many people will prefer *ex-boyfriend* to *exboyfriend* but *expatriate* over *ex-patriate*. The Latin prefix *co-* is similar in many ways. Some argue that sound should be what determines it; others say Latin spelling should determine it.

To write *cooperate* is not wrong, but many prefer to separate the *co* with a hyphen to emphasise the *co-* portion of the 'joint participation' function of *co-* as well as to prevent confusion over pronunciation. Shakespeare used the word *co-mate* in his works. Without the hyphen one might understandably read it as *comate* (like "comet"). Another example is *co-op* ("co-op"), which some prefer to write *coop*. This is bound to be confused with *coop*, as in "coop". There are also some exceptions: *coerce* and *coexist* are usually spelt as such.

The American approach has long been to do away with hyphens as much as possible and go the Latin way, without a hyphen. While American English prefers *cooperation*, *coordinal* etc. based on this rule, for some reason it still prefers *co-opt*. Funny, then, that this word comes from the Latin *cooptare*, which clearly doesn't use a hyphen. As you can see, there is inconsistency.

This may all seem trivial but – if only for sanity's sake –maintaining consistency is commonly achieved through "house style" – and house styles do vary. However, when it comes to British and American spelling there are two clear patterns of choice exist: American English traditionally leans towards *coo-* spellings; and British English traditionally leans strongly towards *co-o-* spellings.

The important thing to remember is to be consistent in your choice of spelling. Even if you go for *coo-* spellings, here is a list of words to consider retaining the hyphen in:

✓ co-agent
✓ co-chair
✓ co-conspirator
✓ co-determination
✓ co-editor
✓ co-financed
✓ co-host
✓ co-occur
✓ co-operate
✓ co-operative
✓ co-opt
✓ co-ordinate
✓ co-ordination
✓ co-partner
✓ co-portion
✓ co-producer
✓ co-star
✓ co-worship

✓ co-author
✓ co-counsel
✓ co-dependant
✓ co-ed
✓ co-education
✓ co-founder
✓ co-latitude
✓ co-op
✓ co-operation
✓ co-operator
✓ co-ordinal
✓ co-ordinance
✓ co-owner
✓ co-payment
✓ co-pilot
✓ co-signatory
✓ co-worker
✓ co-write

# 51

## years'/minutes'/months'

### *We'll have hours and hours of fun*

✓ **five hours' access**
✗ *five hours access*
✓ **3 months' work**
✗ *3 months work*
✓ **two years' training**
✗ *two years training*

✓ **10 weeks' time**
✗ *10 weeks time*
✓ **2 hours' free parking**
✗ *2 hours free parking*
✓ **several lifetimes' worth**
✗ *several lifetimes worth*

**Write *an hour's work, a day's labour, a month's worth, a year's salary* etc. for expressing a single unit of time duration; and *five hours', 10 days', many months', several years'* etc., when expressing multiples.**

There are two ways to express time:

Let's meet back here in two hours.
Let's meet back here in two hours' time.
It will be ready in an hour.
It will be ready in an hour's time.
We will look back in 100 years' time and wonder how we managed.
We will look back in 100 years and wonder how we managed.

The difference between needing and not needing an apostrophe after, say *years*, depends on whether or not you are expressing units or quantity or duration of time.

I am 10 years old.
= *units, quantity (expressing the number of years, but not time)*
He was sentenced to 10 years' imprisonment.
= *duration of time (expressing 10 years of imprisonment)*

This word *of* is key here because it can serve as a useful reminder that it is being used to express "how much *of* something":

There is going to be 10 cm of snow.

The council bought five tonnes of grit and salt.
This part-time course is taking up so much of my time.

Remove *of* from these and an apostrophe is needed. Compare these two examples:

**✓ I am going to need two hours' access.**
**✓ I am going to need two hours of access.**

The only difference between these is that *of* has been removed. English speakers have developed a shorthand and stripped *of* from certain expressions, especially when it comes to time. It is this missing *of* that the apostrophe represents (like in *I'm* for *I am*). Advertisers and sign writers are notorious for getting this type of apostrophe wrong. It is incorrect to write:

**✗** *Three months free membership*
**✗** *Win two days free access*
**✗** *2 hours free parking*

The way to make correct plural forms of duration is simply to write *months'* and *months of*. Both are equally valid and correct.
  The above examples should, of course, be written as:

**✓ Three months' free membership**
**✓ Three months of free membership**
**✓ Win two days' free access**
**✓ Win two days of free access**
**✓ 2 hours' free parking**
**✓ 2 hours of free parking**

Likewise, the following examples in the singular are all correct:

**✓ one hour's notice**
**✓ an honest day's work**
**✓ in one day's time**
**✓ one month's salary**
**✓ a year's benefit**

Units of more than one are always expressed as plurals, with an -*s* that denotes plural, followed by the apostrophe to make -*s'* (though never with -*s's*). With *worth* and *time*, this gives us:

**✓ 3 months' worth**          **✓ five hours' worth**
**✗** *3 months worth*          **✗** *five hours worth*

120

✓ **two years' worth**          ✓ **several lifetimes' worth**
✗ *two years worth*            ✗ *several lifetimes worth*
✓ **in 10 days' time**          ✓ **in five years' time**
✗ *in 10 days time*            ✗ *in five years time*

To express singular units of time duration write [*time*] + -*'s*. This gives us:

✓ **a moment's notice**
✓ **a second's glance**
✓ **a minute's progress**
✓ **an extra day's holiday**
✓ **it is one hour's journey away**
✓ **an hour's exercise**
✓ **in one day's time**
✓ **1 month's worth**
✓ **a year's worth**
✓ **a lifetime's worth**

Note: the word *worth* needs a possessive apostrophe even though it is not related to time.

✓ **I want my money's worth.**
✓ **a DVD's worth of data**
✓ **a whole bucket's worth**

# 52

## mid-
### *Going mad about mid season*

| | |
|---|---|
| ✓ **Mid-season sale** | ✓ **Mid-1960s** |
| ✗ *Mid season sale* | ✗ *Mid 1960s* |
| ✗ *Midseason sale* | |
| ✓ **Mid-life crisis** | ✓ **Midsummer** |
| ✗ *Mid life crisis* | ✗ *Mid-summer* |

**Make sure to write *mid-* and not *mid*, which is not a word in its own right.**

Take a walk down the high streets of Britain and it won't take long before you come across signs such as 'MID SEASON SALE'. The mistake is that *mid* needs a hyphen.

> ✓ **Mid-season sale**
> ✗ *Mid season sale*

There are many *mid-* words; most have hyphens and some do not, but *mid* should not appear alone.

> ✓ **He stopped me in mid-conversation.**
> ✗ *He stopped me in mid conversation.*
> ✓ **The book will be out in mid-October.**
> ✗ *The book will be out in mid October.*
> ✓ **It must be a mid-life crisis.**
> ✗ *It must be a midlife crisis.*
> ✓ **The planes collided in mid-air.**
> ✗ *The planes collided in mid air.*

The occasional place name uses *Mid* on its own (with a capital), like *Mid Glamorgan* and *Mid Wales* but these are exceptions. *Mid Atlantic* is American English for *mid-Atlantic*. It is only ever spelt *'mid* with an apostrophe in poetry, which short for *amid*, rather than *middle*.

Some established words (but not all) are fused as one word, without a hyphen:

✓ midwife                    ✓ midsection
✓ midfield/er                ✓ midsummer
✓ midwinter                  ✓ midweek

Hyphenation can become confusing if over analysed. Just don't leave them out because you are unsure. (For more about joined-up words, see also **44**, **53**, **54**, **63**, **81** and **90**.)

# 53

## up to date versus up-to-date
### *It's up to you to be up to date*

✓ **My accounts are up to date.**
✗ *My accounts are up-to-date.*
✓ **I have enclosed an up-to-date CV/résumé.**
✗ *I have enclosed an up to date CV/résumé.*

**Use *up-to-date* when it describes another word, such as *up-to-date menu*, otherwise write that something is *up to date*.**

The hyphens are used to form what are called compound words. (For more about joined-up words, see also **44**, **52**, **54**, **63**, **81** and **90**.)

# 54

## full time versus full-time
### *A solution to a full-time problem*

✓ **I work part time.**
✗ *I work part-time.*
✓ **I am looking for a full-time job.**
✗ *I am looking for a full time job.*
✓ **He is also a part-time photographer.**
✗ *He is also a part time photographer.*

**The difference between *full time* and *full-time* is that the hyphenated one describes what comes after it. The unhyphenated version does not describe anything, so no hyphen is needed.**

The following are all correct:

✓ **You will work on the project full time for the next month.**
✓ **He is a full-time photographer.**
✓ **I would ideally like full-time work.**
✓ **He is coming back on a part-time basis.**
✓ **I am only looking for a part-time job/role/position.**
✓ **I work on a full-time basis.**
✓ **We need to employ a part-time consultant.**
✓ **They both work part time.**
✓ **I worked there full time for six years.**
✓ **We want you to come and work for us full time.**

Look closely and you will see that all of the hyphenated examples are linked to form a description of the word directly after it. If nothing is being described then you can play it safe without using a hyphen.

Using them the wrong way round on a recruitment advert looks unprofessional. Doing so in your CV/résumé or covering letter could make a world of difference – all because of a tiny line of ink. (For more about joined-up words, see also **44**, **52**, **53**, **63**, **81** and **90**.)

# 55

## learned versus learnt
### *How is 'spelled' spelt?*

**American spelling permits only *learned, burned, spelled*
spellings while British English employs both the *spelled*,
*leaped* and *spelt, leapt* systems of spelling.**

Two things are certain, however. The *-t* form is recognised by all as a
chiefly British form and the *-ed* forms are the required form in American
English. There is a group of verbs that cause people a great deal of confusion, namely those that can be spelt either *-ed* (regular) or *-t* (irregular).
There are 11 main verbs belonging to this class, as well as the addition of
the verbs *light* and *knit*:

> *burn, dream, dwell, kneel, lean, leap, learn, smell, spell, spill* and
> *spoil*; *knit* and *light*

These 13 are the focus of problems in the matter of *-ed* versus *-t* spellings. The good news for those using *American English* is that they are
almost universally spelled with *-ed* endings, including a strong preference
for *lighted*. However, *kneeled* and *knelt* are equally valid (although *knelt*
dominates) and *dwelt* is standard in the US.

The *-ed/-t* dilemma remains a largely *British* (Commonwealth) *English*
one. It also has a problem of it own making: trends in British English
have slowly drifted away from what was once exclusively *-ed* and *-ed(e)*
towards the newer *-t* spellings; it is American English that stayed loyal to
the traditional *-ed* forms.

What we have today is the following situation:

**AMERICAN ENGLISH**
- ✓ **burned, dreamed, dwelt, knelt (and kneeled), leaned, leaped,
learned, lit, knitted (and knit), smelled, spelled, spilled,
spoiled.**
- ✗ *burnt, dreamt, leant, leapt, learnt, lighted, smelt, spelt, spilt, spoilt.*

**BRITISH ENGLISH**
✓ burnt, dreamt, dwelt, knelt, leant, leapt, learnt, lit, knit, smelt, spelt, spilt, spoilt.
✓ burned, dreamed, dwelt, kneeled (and knelt), leaned, leaped, learned, lighted (and lit), knit (and knitted), smelled, spelled, spilled, spoiled.

Stepping back for a moment, overall trend in English is for verbs that are moving towards fully irregular (i.e. *-t*) forms. Today we have *keep → kept*, *deal → dealt, feel → felt, sleep → slept* and *mean → meant*, where they once had *-ed(e)* (regular) endings. According to findings presented in *One Language, Two Grammars*, by Cambridge University Press, the transition from regular to irregular typically takes 300 years. *Spoilt* first appeared in the 1600s and *knelt* appeared in the 1800s. *Lit* has gained ground on *lighted* since the 1800s and may one day replace it fully.

The advance of *-t* forms is very much a British phenomenon in the case of the 13 verbs in question, which are in transition. The *-ed* forms are holding their own in American English, whereas their *speed→sped* (instead of the British speeded), *plead→pled* (instead of *pleaded*) are gaining ground there. Academics also have noted that the *-t* forms in British English are closely linked with formal and conservative styles of writing.

Therefore, contrary to popular, "educated" opinion, spellings such as *learnt* are actually the preferred forms in formal British English; not *learned*, which is now more a characteristic of American spelling. (The same is true of *lit* (as in *a lit candle* or *a lit room*), *lighted* is more characteristic of American English.) This popular falsehood, it would seem, may be linked to the misconceived association with the participle adjective *learned*, as in *learned fellow*. Because of this one term, a lot of people in Britain will make a song and dance, reject *learnt* and always insist on *learned*. What they will then ignore, however, is how the rest of the 12 verbs in this category are spelled/spelt.

While the Americans are adamant about keeping these mostly consistent and reject strongly the *-t* forms, British spelling unfortunately remains in constant flux, with writers switching indiscriminately between *-ed* and *-t* across the set without concern for consistency.

## CONSISTENCY IS KEY

Nothing better illustrates the haphazard inconsistency of *-ed/-t* spellings in British English than looking at a range of dictionaries and how these do little to improve the situation.

From a writer's position, the best practice is to choose one form, stick to it and be consistent. We all know that British spelling permits only *-our* forms (*colour*, *honour*, *valour* etc.) and that American English permits *-or* of these same words. Instead of a mishmash approach of *color* here, *valour* there, and *honor* else where, we spell them consistently – and our dictionaries follow suit.

It is interesting then, to observe that similar concern is not taken with the treatment of *-ed* and *-t* spellings in British English. Nor are dictionaries consistent in their approach. Unlike regional *-our* and *-or* spellings, *-ed* and *-t* are left to personal preference by individual writers, publications, house styles and – crucially – by our dictionaries.

Even though all dictionaries recognise that *-t* forms are exclusively the reserve of British English and that academics have demonstrated that these forms are frequently linked to formal British English, it is both fascinating and frustrating to observe because, if our dictionaries are of no help with regard to certain spellings, how else do we know how to spell them? It is bizarre that British writers have two parallel choices, though not one dictionary gives these 13 verbs equal and consistent treatment.

We all understand that when dictionaries present words with variable spellings that the preferred spelling always appears first and that any variations appear second, often in brackets. The implication is that we interpret the first spelling as the "correct", "primary" or "preferred" one. Not only are dictionaries inconsistent with their preferred spelling of this word class, they appear to chop and change with each new edition over time.

To begin with, the *Oxford English Dictionary* prefers *-t* spellings first for 7 out of 13 of these verbs in its 2006, *Concise* edition. While it gave 9 in the 1992 edition, which would suggest that with time the direction has pushed back towards *-ed* forms. Online, however, on the *askoxford* website, it gives 8 *-t* spellings first, reinstating *burnt*, *dreamt* and *spelt*, and describes *kneeled* as a chiefly US spelling. After long support for *dwelt*, the advice online is for *dwelled* to be preferred.

| Oxford dictionaries | burnt | dreamt | dwelt | knelt | knit | leant | leapt | learnt | lit | smelt | spelt | spilt | spoilt |
|---|---|---|---|---|---|---|---|---|---|---|---|---|---|
| askoxford.com (2010) | ✓ | ✓ | ✓ | | | | | | ✓ | ✓ | ✓ | ✓ | ✓ |
| OED (2010) | | | ✓ | ✓ | | | | | ✓ | ✓ | | ✓ | ✓ |
| Concise (2006) | | | ✓ | ✓ | | | | | ✓ | ✓ | | ✓ | ✓ |
| OED (1992) | ✓ | ✓ | ✓ | ✓ | | | | | ✓ | ✓ | ✓ | ✓ | ✓ |

By contrast, the *Chambers* dictionaries look completely different. The *Paperback* version, published in 2007, gives *-t* spellings first billing in 10 out of 12 verbs (it has no entry for *dwelt/dwelled* whatsoever) and puts *spoiled* first.

From this perspective, given its strong preference for *-t* forms, it is more interesting to discover that Chambers' full, hardback edition from 2008 gives *-t* spellings first choice in only 2 out of 13 words. For some reason, only *burnt* and *dwelt* have first billing. It then gives the advice that the *-t* form *spoilt* should be used only when describing "damage" or "ruin" (i.e. *spoilt vote* and *spoiled child*), and *spoiled* for "indulge" – since its 1978 version – something that no other English dictionary does.

Meanwhile, an online search of its free web dictionary – which uses the *Chambers 21st Century Dictionary* – gives something different again: 9 out of 13 are *-t* forms, the exceptions being *burned*, *dreamed* and *smelled* – almost the mirror opposite of its print edition. It gives preference to *knitted* but describes *knit* as belonging to 'old use'. It gives *spoilt* as the first choice and makes no mention of *spoiled* having the exclusive meaning of "ruined".

| Chambers dictionaries | burnt | dreamt | dwelt | knelt | knit | leant | leapt | learnt | lit | smelt | spelt | spilt | spoilt |
|---|---|---|---|---|---|---|---|---|---|---|---|---|---|
| Chambers (2008) | ✓ | | ✓ | | | | | | | | | | |
| Chambers paperback (2007) | ✓ | | – | ✓ | | ✓ | ✓ | | | ✓ | ✓ | ✓ | ✓ |
| Chambers (online) | | | ✓ | ✓ | ✓ | ✓ | ✓ | | ✓ | | ✓ | ✓ | ✓ |
| Chambers 21st Cent. (1978) | ✓ | | ✓ | | | | | | | | | | |

The Collins dictionaries are far more consistent, adopting a near uniform preference for *-t* forms in the 1986 dictionary, the only exceptions being *knitted* and *lighted*. From that point onwards it switches in favour of *leaned* and *learned*, yet stays with *leapt* for no apparent reason. *Dreamed*, too, gets changed but returns in 2009 when *dreamt* regained first preference.

| Collins dictionaries | burnt | dreamt | dwelt | knelt | knit | leant | leapt | learnt | lit | smelt | spelt | spilt | spoilt |
|---|---|---|---|---|---|---|---|---|---|---|---|---|---|
| collinslanguage.com | ✓ | | ✓ | ✓ | | | | ✓ | | ✓ | | ✓ | ✓ |
| Collins (2009) (UK) | ✓ | ✓ | ✓ | ✓ | | | | ✓ | | ✓ | ✓ | ✓ | ✓ |
| Collins (1999) | ✓ | | ✓ | ✓ | | | | ✓ | | ✓ | ✓ | ✓ | ✓ |
| Collins Paperback (1986) | ✓ | ✓ | ✓ | ✓ | | ✓ | ✓ | ✓ | | ✓ | ✓ | ✓ | ✓ |
| collinslanguage.com | ✓ | | ✓ | ✓ | | | | ✓ | | ✓ | ✓ | ✓ | ✓ |

The Penguin dictionaries seem to have recently shifted from favouring -*ed* forms towards -*t* forms. After headlining only four -*t* forms in the 2002 paperback edition, the comprehensive hardback edition published in 2007 doubles this to eight after it adopted *dwelt*, *smelt*, *spelt* and *spoilt*. It briefly adopted *knitted* in 2004 but soon took back *knit* as its preferred form – the only British dictionary to sanction this form.

| Penguin dictionaries | burnt | dreamt | dwelt | knelt | knit | leant | leapt | learnt | lit | smelt | spelt | spilt | spoilt |
|---|---|---|---|---|---|---|---|---|---|---|---|---|---|
| Penguin dictionary (2007) | | | ✓ | ✓ | ✓ | | | | | ✓ | ✓ | ✓ | ✓ |
| Penguin concise (2004) | | | ✓ | ✓ | | | | | | ✓ | | ✓ | ✓ |
| Concise dictionary (2002) | | | ✓ | ✓ | | | | | | | | ✓ | |

The Longman online (www.ldoceonline.com) dictionary does make some effort to distinguish between British and American spelling preferences, though it does not take a uniform approach with all 13 verbs. Only five are specifically listed with separate American spellings, while British spellings get varying descriptions. It gives *knelt* first billing and specifically adds that it is also *kneeled* in American English, it favours *leaned* as first spelling but notes that it is also *learnt* "especially British English"; the same is used for *learned* and *learnt*. *Leapt*, *smelt*, *spelt* and *spilt* are described as British English and *leaped*, *smelled*, *spelled* and *spilled* are described as American English. *Spoiled* is given first billing but again, the alternative *spoilt* is described as British English.

| Longman dictionaries | burnt | dreamt | dwelt | knelt | knit | leant | leapt | learnt | lit | smelt | spelt | spilt | spoilt |
|---|---|---|---|---|---|---|---|---|---|---|---|---|---|
| Longman online | ✓ | | ✓ | ✓ | | | ✓ | ✓ | ✓ | ✓ | ✓ | | |

The Cambridge online dictionary gives yet more variation: only 5 out 13 verbs are given -*t* forms as first preference. Their choices are noteworthy because they are among the few who appear to reject -*t* spellings for the words *smelled*, *spelled*, *spilled* and *spoiled*.

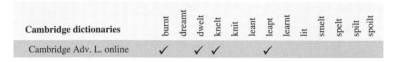

| Cambridge dictionaries | burnt | dreamt | dwelt | knelt | knit | leant | leapt | learnt | lit | smelt | spelt | spilt | spoilt |
|---|---|---|---|---|---|---|---|---|---|---|---|---|---|
| Cambridge Adv. L. online | ✓ | ✓ | ✓ | | | ✓ | | | | | | | |

Last, one confusing piece of advice comes not from a dictionary but the *Longman Guide to English Usage* (1992), which is a British book. Under *burned* and *burnt*, it gives the advice that *burned* be the choice when the verb has no object (*the flame burned brightly*), for both British and American English. It then gives the advice that where the verb *does* has an object, *burnt* be used for British English (*the boy burnt his fingers*) and *burned* be used for American (*the boy burned his fingers*). Not only that, it further gives the advice that *burnt* be used as the *adjective* – in both American and British English (*she has burnt skin*). For *knit*, it recommends *knitted* for things made of yarn (*knitted socks*) and *knit* for "united" (*a closely knit group*).

While none of the above explanations appear in any other dictionaries, some have also argued that -*ed* forms are frequent (in British English) when there is suggestion of duration (*we looked on as the house burned*), while -*t* forms have a tendency to express "punctual" events (*I burnt my toast*). Others have argued that this makes sense also on the grounds that one sounds longer than the other. But these theories have not proved conclusive, although research has found that it is somewhat evident in the British press. It does not explain why they do not occur in US English.

## FINAL THOUGHTS

Although this chapter goes into some depth, the point of this close examination of a range of dictionaries is to illustrate just how chaotic the situation is with -*ed* and -*nt* in regard to the traditional tool of advice – the dictionary – and how great inconsistencies exist in British English.

Two things are certain, however. The -*t* form is recognised by all as a chiefly British form and the -*ed* forms are the required form in American English.

On a personal note, I associate -*t* forms with British English and have a strong preference for them, which is why I have used them throughout this book. As for the American forms, I admire that there exists a uniform approach. This serves only to give American writers a – if only small – sense of certainty about being confident spellers. I can only hope that this, too, will one day be the case for British English, one way or the other. Likewise, we can only hope that British dictionaries lead the way and take a less random attitude to the spelling of these 13 verbs in the future so that they get straightened out once and for all.

Oh, and *earned* is never spelt *earnt* – at least not for the next 100 years...

# 56

## led versus lead

*As good as a led balloon*

✓ **The discovery led to a revolution in science.**
✗ *The discovery lead to a revolution in science.*
✓ **They led the convoy towards the border.**
✗ *They lead the convoy towards the border.*

### The past tense of *to lead* is *led*, not *lead*.

It is unfortunate that *lead* is both a verb that rhymes with *bleed* and a poisonous metal that rhymes with *head* – and that *led* sounds like the metal and vice versa. Nor is it helpful when *leading* is both a typographical term for line spacing ("leding") and a type of role played by an actor ("leeding").

These illogical variances in pronunciation are probably the cause of so many people incorrectly writing *lead* when they mean, *led*. The same is also true of *mislead* and *misled*.

✓ **The group leader led the way.**
✗ *The group leader lead the way.*
✓ **I don't think that he misled you on purpose.**
✗ *I don't think that he mislead you on purpose.*

# 60

## proved versus proven
### *A proven confusion*

✓ **There is no way that it can be done, we have proved it.**
✗ *There is no way that it can be done, we have proven it.*
✓ **He has really proved himself this week.**
✗ *He has really proven himself this week.*
✓ **There is absolutely no way that this allegation can be proved.**
✗ *There is absolutely no way that this allegation can be proven.*
✓ **That is an allegation that has yet to be proved.**
✗ *That is an allegation that has yet to be proven.*

✓ **proven benefits**
✓ **proven ability**
✓ **scientifically proven properties**
✗ *scientifically proved properties*

**There is a difference in meaning between *proved* and *proven*. The correct past tense form of the verb *prove* is *proved*. This is the case in both British English and American English, while *proven* is used as an adjective to describe a noun ("thing").**

✓ **The house purchase has proved problematic.**
✗ *The house purchase has proven problematic.*
✓ **The house has a proven structural problem.**

To start with the history of this conundrum, *proven* originates from a legal term from Scots law, namely *not proven*. It was used strictly in this sense for a long time. It then crossed the Atlantic and into American English, where it widened to become the colloquial past tense of *prove*. It has since been on the rise in British English but has never eclipsed the correct form *proved*. It remains informal in the US too, in both active (*he has proven*) and passive (*it is not yet proven*) constructions.

The following are correct:

✓ **We have already proved it.**
✗ *We have already proven it.*
✓ **We have proved our theory to be correct.**
✗ *We have proven our theory to be correct.*
✓ **That allegation simply cannot be proved.**
✗ *That allegation simply cannot be proven.*
✓ **We are innocent until proved guilty.**
✗ *We are innocent until proven guilty.*
✓ **I think that they have already proved that.**
✗ *I think that they have already proven that.*
✓ **Would you say that you have proved yourself?**
✗ *Would you say that you have proven yourself?*
✓ **Their prediction proved correct.**
✗ *Their prediction proven correct.*

Although some dictionaries include *proven* as an alternative to *proved*, the latter remains the only choice for good writers, editors and publications.

While some will claim that *not proven* is accepted as standard English in legal documents, it remains a legal formula restricted strictly to Scots law; not English law, which has a separate legal system altogether. It should not be used instead of *not proved* in a general sense.

As an adjective, *proven* has proved more useful, though many traditionalists still avoid it because it is close to being a cliche. Personally, I think that it is here to stay.

✓ **I have a proven track record in generating sales.**
✓ **It is a well proven model**
✓ **proven track record**
✓ **proven reserves**
✓ **proven winner**
✓ **proven technology**

It is interesting, too, from an observational point of view to witness the discord between the attitudes towards *proven* as a verb and *gotten*, which has established itself widely throughout the US and Australia when it comes to the correct form *got* (preferred in the UK). Many Britons dislike *gotten* but lack the same passionate feelings when it comes to *proven*.

On a final note, *proven* (even when used incorrectly instead of *proved*) should not rhyme with "woven" under any circumstances. This is nothing but hypercorrect, posed nonsense.

# 61

## presently versus currently
### *The present is currently unavailable*

✓ **A forensic team is currently investigating the murder scene.**
✗ *A forensic team is presently investigating the murder scene.*
✓ **There is currently a long waiting list for that product.**
✗ *There is presently a long waiting list for that product.*

**Write *currently* instead of *presently* to mean, "at this time" or "now", and *current* instead of *present*. Use *presently* only to mean, "soon".**

The mistake that people frequently make is to write *presently* when they actually mean, *currently*. The problem perhaps comes from the association with *at present*, which as an adverb is *currently*.

✓ **This target is currently not achievable.**
✗ *This target is presently not achievable.*
✓ **What are you working on currently?**
✗ *What are you working on presently?*

The trouble with *presently* is that its meaning differs from person to person. It means either "soon" or "now" – quite opposite meanings – depending on where in the English-speaking world you live, which is why both meanings are unhelpfully described in various dictionaries.

The standard meaning of *presently* in British English is "soon" or "shortly". A second – older – meaning of "now" or "immediately" is more common in Scotland and the US, but not standard in either. This meaning ceased being standard around the 1600s. If it died off 400 years ago, it must have been for a good reason. The best advice is to avoid using this second meaning in formal British English – it causes only confusion, even if it is understood in the US.

✓ **The store is closing presently (US).**
✓ **The store is closing soon (UK).**

That said, even when used in the standard sense, as in *We will be landing presently*, many people prefer *shortly*, *soon* or *in a moment*. Some argue that there is no need to use *presently* at all. I agree.

On a related topic, the word *momentarily* causes similar problems. In the US it means "soon" or "shortly" – occupying the first meaning of *presently* – whereas in British English it is understood to mean, "for a brief moment".

> (UK) I spoke to him momentarily.
> (US) We will be landing momentarily.

The same principle applies to *present* ant *current*. Discerning communicators avoid using *present* in the adjectival sense *now*, which they prefer to express as *current*. Doing so leaves *present* to mean, *in place* and *at present* to mean, *now*.

> ✓ **I got a phone call from the current manager.**
> ✗ *I got a phone call from the present manager.*
> ✓ **She is the current correspondent.**
> ✗ *She is the present correspondent.*
> ✓ **She is the only correspondent present in the area.**
> ✓ **The moisture present in the fabric will cause rot.**
> ✓ **We are not currently offering that service.**
> ✓ **We are not offering that service at present.**
> ✗ *We are not presently offering that service.*

# 62

## myriad
### *A myriad of abuse*

✓ **They face myriad uncertainties.**
✓ **I am absolutely fascinated by the myriad stars in the universe.**
✗ *The town has a myriad of gangs – no fewer than 130.*

**Careful writers restrict *myriad* to mean, "countless/infinite in number". Take care when using it as a noun.**

*Myriad* is a great word with poetic and literary connotations. However, it is used so frequently and so casually for everything that it risks being overused and becoming hackneyed.

Deriving from Greek *muriad-,* from earlier *murios*, meaning, "10,000", the modern-day meaning of *myriad* is "countless" or "indefinite/great in number". It came into use as an adjective during the 1800s, causing a lot of confusion ever since.

✓ **We are sure to encounter myriad setbacks and obstacles.**
✗ *We are sure to encounter a myriad of setbacks and obstacles.*

First, this strictly traditional sense of *myriad* is used where the exact number is not – or cannot – be known, i.e. when it is impossible to know just what or how many setbacks and obstacles (if any) are going to be faced. In this sense, too, this use of *myriad* stirs the imagination with the rhetorical reference to the unknown. This is how traditionalists would prefer that it remained.

In looser terms, careful writers dislike when *myriad* is used as a synonym of *countless* and *multifaceted/multidimensional – in myriad ways. Myriad* is wrong when it uses the noun form, *a myriad of*. Instead, use it exactly as you would *many*.

✓ **The pyramids were built using myriad stone blocks.**
✗ *The pyramids were built using a myriad of stone blocks.*

Purists also avoid using it as a noun, similar to *a range of*. Used in this way it requires *a myriad of*.

> ✓ **They will address a myriad of ethical and environmental issues.**
> ✓ **We are bombarded daily with a myriad of advertising messages.**

So, while the traditionalist's view is that it should be used only as an adjective (to describe things) and not as a noun, not everyone agrees. Usage authorities dismiss it on both sides of the Atlantic. There is nothing wrong, as such, with using it as a noun – it has a long history to back it up.

The real danger, however, is when *myriad* is used as a lazy synonym of plain old *many*:

> ✗ *The new machine features a myriad of buttons.*
> ✗ *She counts being a mum among her myriad achievements.*
> ✗ *The new model comes in myriad colours.*
> ✗ *The menu features myriad classic dishes.*

Used like this, the splendour of the word wears quickly; no doubt, the buttons, achievements and colours being suggested are far from 'infinite'. By definition, a menu cannot have *myriad dishes* – these can be counted. On these grounds, those who prefer to restrict its usage as an adjective (without *a* and *of*) for the truly uncountable present a good case. Why subject it to overuse?

Last, we know that *myriad* means "countless or many in number", so there is no need to say so twice:

> ✗ *...a myriad number of...*
> ✗ *...a myriad of different ways...*

# 63

## well versus well-
### *Well, I never!*

✓ **It is a well financed business.**
✗ *It is a well-financed business.*
✓ **I represent a well respected film director.**
✗ *I represent a well-respected film director.*
✓ **They are such well behaved children.**
✗ *They are such well-behaved children.*

**Don't shy away from using the adverb *well* in the correct way – without a hyphen.**

Just when you understood the difference between a *small-business plan* and *a small business plan* (see **90**) and why *freshly squeezed OJ* does not need a hyphen (see **43**), along comes an exception. Actually, this is not an exception. Contrary to popular belief, no hyphen is required after *well* in, for example, *a well respected person*. This is because the adverb *well* describes *respected*, not *person*.

Don't be surprised if you find that this advice even goes against what your teachers and English books have told you. No doubt many of you are frowning right now and need more convincing, while some of you may even be about to blow a fuse at what I am suggesting, but let's look at the situation a little closer:

a man

Bear with me for perhaps being over simple. Here we start with a noun (a thing or object), in this example *a man*.

a poor man
an educated man

Now we have described him as a *poor* man as well as an *educated* man. Both words are adjectives; words that describe nouns. When he is both poor *and* educated, we would string them together with a comma.

a poor, educated man

*Poor* does not describe *educated*. Both words still describe *man*. If we want to describe 'how poor' or 'how educated', we use adverbs.

a poorly educated man
a really poor man

Here, *poorly* describes *educated*, not *man*. Likewise *really* describes *poor*, not 'man'. This is also what *well* does:

a fully funded course
a well funded course
a lightly salted meal
a well salted meal

So, believe it or not, there is no need to use hyphen.

&#10003; **a well built man**
&#10007; *a well-built man*
&#10003; **a well known man**
&#10007; *a well-known man*
&#10003; **a well educated man**
&#10007; *a well-educated man*

All of these are correct:

&#10003; **a well financed project**
&#10003; **a brilliantly orchestrated project**
&#10003; **a well respected author**
&#10003; **a critically acclaimed author**
&#10003; **a well known country**
&#10003; **a badly run country**
&#10003; **a well packed bag**
&#10003; **a neatly packed bag**
&#10003; **a well assembled team**
&#10003; **a hastily assembled team**
&#10003; **a well managed operation**
&#10003; **a badly managed operation**

Those of you who have reached for your reference books will probably read something along the lines that, in "well-dressed person", "well + dressed" describes "person" so it needs a hyphen because this is a "compound adjective". What is being overlooked here, however, is that *well* is an adverb, not an adjective; and *adverbs* describe *actions*, not *things* (nouns).

However, as we have seen above, no hyphens are needed because these are all adverbs. Therefore, no compound hyphen is needed when an adverb describes a verb. A *university-educated man* is a compound adjective, and requires a hyphen.

Most will agree that a *newly made suit* does not need a hyphen (because *newly* (an adverb) describes *made*, not the *suit*) and that a *tailor-made suit* does require one (because *tailor + made* describes the *suit*). *Newly* is an adverb. *Well* is an adverb too (*well* the adjective means "good in health" and *well* the noun is "a source of water"). Therefore, a *well made suit* does not require a hyphen because *well* describes *made*, not the *suit*.

> a tailor-made suit = *tailor + made describes the suit*
> *(tailor is not an adverb)*
> a hand-made suit = *hand + made also describes the suit*
> *(hand is not an adverb)*
> a well made suite = *well describes how well the suit is made*
> *(well is an adverb)*

This is why I urge you not to shy away from dropping the hyphen in *well-written English* (*sic*). You may become a well known writer for more reasons than one.

Nevertheless, many writers and publications use *well-* instead of *well* in spite of the evidence. And before you say, "This is an example of how language changes, so we should adopt it", this does not change that *well* is an adverb. Until we also accept *beautifully-painted portrait* as correct (see **43**), the spots on the leopard have not changed.

Until recently, one of the few souls brave enough to make mention of the hyphenless *well* had been the *Timesonline* style guide. One of its editors rightly pointed out that no hyphen is needed, but wrote something to the effect that you might as well put the (incorrect) hyphen in because so many people do it – and at least it "looks right". When even the *Times* style editors fear using correct grammar in public, what hope is there for the rest of us? (Since finishing this book the site has since been rewritten and it now advises to always use *well-* "with adjective", "before the noun". It then adds a link to "see Adverbs", which is confusing to say the least.

As a final point, one other problem surrounding *well* is how to treat *more well* and *most well* (such as in "most well known"). The unanimous advice is to change these to *better* and *best* respectively.

> ✓ **The agent wished his client list included some better known names.**
>
> ✗ *The agent wished his client list included some more well known names.*
>
> ✓ **He is the best dressed man in town.**
>
> ✗ *He is the most well dressed man in town.*

(For more about joined-up words, see also **44**, **52**, **53**, **54**, **81** and **90**.)

# 64

## commonly misspelt words
### *make your own Dan Quayle moment*

**Let's be honest, no one gets it right 100% of the time.**

It is wierd how we sometimes think a word definately looks right but regretably we omitt a letter in an akward place and without propper assesment someone else recieves it and spots thows errors, forcing us to make appologies worthy of a tradgedy.

Typos happen. Spelling mistakes, however, are less forgivable. They are more embarrassing because we fail to notice what everyone else does. How many spelling errors did you notice in the preseding, I mean, *preceding*, paragraph?

Even if you spotted all (11) of them, it may still pay to brush up your skills by reviewing this list of commonly misspelt English words for the answers. Learn to identify the words that you frequently get wrong. Keep a list. And practise. Don't just rely on your spell checker to be set up correctly, or – for that matter – set to 'on'.

We all have words that we find difficult to spell, for our own reasons. (My brain always wants to put a second *-s-* in *disappoint*.) But spelling gets better only with practise and by having a good dictionary on hand.

Here is a list of frequently abused words:

| | |
|---|---|
| ✓ accommodate | ✓ achieve |
| ✓ ageing (aging US) | ✓ amok |
| ✓ apologise | ✓ archaeologist |
| ✓ Arctic | ✓ artefact |
| ✓ assessment | ✓ attuned |
| ✓ awkward | ✓ barbecue |
| ✓ Bellwether | ✓ bias |
| ✓ biased | ✓ bigoted |
| ✓ breadth | ✓ burglary |
| ✓ budgeted | ✓ cemetery |
| ✓ clientele | ✓ collapsible |
| ✓ congratulations | ✓ councillor |
| ✓ defendant | ✓ definite |
| ✓ definitely | ✓ desperate |

✓ deterred
✓ dissociate
✓ embarrassed
✓ feasible
✓ focusing
✓ fulfil
✓ gases (plural noun)
✓ gypsy
✓ icicle
✓ instalment
✓ interrupt
✓ italic
✓ kidnapped
✓ laboratory
✓ medieval
✓ mis-sell
✓ necessary
✓ occurrence
✓ oneself
✓ panicked
✓ phial
✓ potatoes
✓ primitive
✓ queue
✓ regrettable
✓ reminisce
✓ resistible
✓ revelry
✓ sanitary
✓ separate
✓ smooths
✓ supersede
✓ targeted
✓ tragedy
✓ vilify
✓ woollen

✓ develop
✓ disused
✓ emphasise
✓ focused
✓ forfeit
✓ fulfilment
✓ gasses (verb)
✓ handfuls
✓ illiberal
✓ intercept
✓ irreparable
✓ itinerary
✓ knick-knack
✓ liaise
✓ miser
✓ misspell
✓ occurred
✓ omitted
✓ opportunity
✓ pastime
✓ potato
✓ preferred
✓ questionnaire
✓ receive
✓ regretted
✓ repetitive
✓ restaurateur
✓ rhythm
✓ sensible
✓ skilful
✓ stupor
✓ tangible
✓ threshold
✓ twelfth
✓ weird
✓ yoghurt

# 65

## historic versus historical
### *An age-old conundrum*

✓ **This item has a lot of historical value.**
✗ *This item has a lot of historic value.*
✓ **These are historic times.**
✗ *These are historical times.*
✓ **It was a historic victory.**
✗ *It was a historical victory.*

**Use *historical* to mean, "true in history", "not fictitious" or "belonging to the past". Use *historic* to mean, "of great significance".**

*Historic* and *historical* are two adjectives that often get confused with one another. The most common mistake is to refer to something happening in the present as being *historical*, which, of course, it cannot yet be if it only just occurred. Therefore, a *historical event* is not the same as a *historic event*. (See **02**, by the way.)

*Historical* should be used exclusively in reference to past events or of things belonging to the past.

✓ **historical accuracy**          ✓ **historical novel**
✓ **historical figure/character**  ✓ **historical perspective**
✓ **historical records**           ✓ **historical drama**
✓ **historical reasons**           ✓ **historical home**

Using *historic* with any of these would greatly alter the meaning, such as the difference between *historic figure* and *historical figure*.

Use *historic* when you mean, "important", "significant" and "momentous" – something that is likely to be recorded in history.

✓ **historic event/moment/day**     ✓ **historic win/victory**
✓ **historic ruling/decision/act**  ✓ **historic visit/step/shift**
✓ **historic site/building**        ✓ **historic level/low/high**

To describe any of the above as *historical* would highlight, not their significance, but their role in earlier times or past events, such as the difference between a *historical event* and a *historic event*.

If anything, *historic* is probably overused. To label something as such is a hackneyed, such as *a historic party*. Whether or not an event or occurrence is important, it will become part of history anyway, just like all past happenings but not all will be remembered.

Sometimes, the cliche even gets pushed to absurd limits, such as *Bad weather forced organisers to call off the historic talks*. They might be important, but they have not yet even happened. Nevertheless, it is still important to use *historic* and *historical* in their proper contexts.

# 66

## meet with/up/to

*Let's not meet up or join with them*

✓ **I met Paul while I was in New York.**
✗ *I met with Paul while I was in New York.*
✗ *I met up with Paul while I was in New York.*
✓ **The minister joined visitors to celebrate.**
✗ *The minister joined with visitors to celebrate.*

**For British English, do not use *meet with*, *speak with*, *chat with*, *consult with* or *join with*. The problem stems from confusing nouns and verbs. Also avoid (or at least, limit) your use of *meet up* and *meet up with*.**

There are some verbs that need the word *with*, but there are also many that don't. While it is correct to write *work with*, *deal with*, *live with*, *agree with* and *struggle with*, American English has recently developed a habit of inserting *with* in places where it is not needed.

| *I will* | meet (with)<br>consult (with)<br>chat (with) | join (with)<br>speak (with) |
|---|---|---|
| *I* | met (with)<br>consulted (with)<br>chatted (with) | joined (with)<br>spoke (with) |

✓ **I am going to meet some consultants tomorrow.**
✗ *I am going to meet with some consultants tomorrow.*

Some will argue that there is a subtle difference between *to meet someone* and *to meet up with someone* claiming that the latter is suitable for brief or unintended encounters – but *meet* still means, "meet", whether it is planned, brief or scheduled. Again, restrict *meet up* to American English where it is more accepted as being correct, yo!

You might, however, *speak with a lisp*, *a stutter* or *a loud voice*. You can book a consultation with a specialist, but you *consult* your specialist, not *consult with*.

| *I speak with:* | a lisp | soft voice |
| | an accent | |
| *I speak to:* | John constantly | every one of my clients |
| | celebrities all of the time | |
| *I will:* | meet | join |
| | consult | speak to |
| | chat to | |
| *I had:* | a meeting with | a consultation with |
| | a chat with | a conversation with |

The problems seem to come from confusion between verbs and nouns. You *meet* a friend, but have *a meeting with* a friend. You *consult* an expert, but book *a consultation with* one. You *chat to* your mum but you have *a chat with* her. You can have a *conversation with* someone but you *speak to* them, not *speak with* them.

✓ **The PM is preparing to meet business leaders tomorrow.**
✗ *The PM is preparing to meet with business leaders tomorrow.*
✓ **The PM is preparing a meeting with business leaders tomorrow.**

Two pieces of wood can be *joined with* glue but you don't say that you will *join with* someone, you simply *join* them.

✓ **I am going to join them tomorrow.**
✗ *I am going to join with them tomorrow.*
✓ **Europe joined the US in condemning the violence.**
✗ *Europe joined with the US in condemning the violence.*

Some of this bad influence undoubtedly comes from American English. While you may get away with writing and speaking this way in the US, and indeed it may be required, it is still frowned on in British English. The same applies when writing *meet up* and *meet up with*, which uses three words instead of just one.

✓ **meet**          ✓ **meet**
✗ *meet up*          ✗ *meet up with*
✓ **engage**
✗ *engage with*

# 67

## And.../But...
### *And the problem is...?*

**There is nothing wrong, incorrect or ungrammatical about starting a sentence with a conjunction, such as *And* or *But*, or ending a sentence with a preposition.**

According to the theory, one should "never, ever start a sentence with a conjunction or end with a preposition" or "never start a sentence with *and* or *but*". This hypercorrect mantra is so ingrained and so widespread in everyday culture – in the UK, the US and the wider English-speaking world – that it is high on the list of written taboos in many peoples' minds. Yet it remains wholly fallacious.

This myth lives despite the number of times that respected authorities on language condemn this "rule" as bogus. And English teachers are arguably the biggest propagators of this nonsense, which is arguably why we are reluctant to go against this "advice".

The fear is that starting a sentence with a preposition makes it an incomplete thought. Prepositions include words like *after*, *through*, *like*, *under* etc. However, prepositions don't just exist as single words. *Except for*, *because of*, *with regard to*, *in spite of* and *apart/aside from* are also prepositions – and how often are they used to start sentences? It is no different with *and* or *but*, which have been used for centuries.

Just to be clear, here are some examples of what we are talking about:

**CONJUNCTIONS**

| | |
|---|---|
| although | and |
| as | but |
| because | for |
| if | or |
| since | though |
| when | while |
| yet | |

If you have ever started a sentence with any of these words then you will have broken the so-called rule. When did you last start a sentence with *when*? Or *while*? So why single out *and* and *but*?

## PREPOSITIONS

| | |
|---|---|
| about | above |
| across | after |
| along | among |
| around | at |
| beside | before |
| below | beyond |
| down | from |
| in | inside |
| of | off |
| on | outside |
| over | past |
| under | up |
| with | without |

If you can't think of how these would ever end a sentence, let me give you some examples:

| | |
|---|---|
| ...in the ground <u>below</u>. | ...in 2020 and <u>beyond</u>. |
| ...in the <u>past</u>. | It is all <u>over</u>. |
| Where are they <u>from</u>? | What did they talk <u>about</u>? |
| I will meet you <u>inside</u>. | Shall we go <u>outside</u>? |

Again, I ask, what is wrong with these? Bernstein sums it up succinctly when he writes: 'People who insist on the rule do not always know about what they are talking. They do not know for what rules are.'

Beginning sentences with prepositions or conjunctions has always been a feature of the English language, from the Anglo-Saxon period onwards. How often do sentences begin with the conjunction *because*? *And* and *but* are also conjunctions. In fact, *and* is among the oldest English words, stemming from Old English *ond* and related to Germanic *und*. It is also the third-most frequent word in the English language. The word *but* also stems from Old English. Both words function perfectly well as introductions. And always have. But don't let anyone tell you otherwise. But just don't overdo it and start every sentence with one.

# 68

## onto versus on to/into versus in to
### *Are you into 'onto'?*

✓ **The burglar broke into the house.**
✗ *The burglar broke in to the house.*
✓ **My friends all came in to say hello.**
✗ *My friends all came into say hello.*
✓ **Amy walked onto the platform.**
✗ *Amy walked on to the platform.*
✓ **I took my hand luggage onto the plane.**
✗ *I took my hand luggage on to the plane.*

**It can be difficult to tell the difference between *into/
in to* and *onto/on to*. First put the fused words into one
category in your mind, and *in to* and *on to* in another. Try
removing *on* or *in* to test if your sentence still makes sense
– if it does, then the split form is usually correct.**

> I drove onto the motorway and once I reached Scotland I drove on to
> Edinburgh.
> My wife came in to kiss me before putting the groceries into the
> fridge.

In the sentences above, *onto* and *on to* become incorrect if they are switched
round; so, too, *in to* and *into*. If the separate *on* and *in* were removed
from each sentence, the meaning would remain the same but contain less
information. You can test the sentence by removing *on* from *onto* and *in*
from *into*; they will usually be split forms if they can be removed without
affecting the sentence.

✓ **My boss came in to speak to me today.**
✓ **My boss came to speak to me today.**
✗ *My boss came into speak to me today.*
✓ **I bumped into the car behind me.**
✗ *I bumped to the car behind me.*
✗ *I bumped in to the car behind me.*

When *in to* and *into* work when reversed round, *into* is often wrong; when *in to* and *into* don't make sense when switched, *into* is usually correct. This is a simplified way to remember which is which of the four alternatives, but it is not foolproof. With *in to,* this rule does not work is with verbs that typically have *in* after them, such as *tune in, flood in, fly in, cave in, tuck in, give in, step in* etc.

✓ **I want to step in to help out.**
✓ **I want to step into the water.**
✓ **The boys climbed onto the roof.**
✓ **The boys climbed on to the roof.**

With *on to* and *onto*, a good test of which is correct comes from testing whether you can fit any additional information between the two words. If you can add words between them without garbling the meaning, then *onto* will usually not be correct:

✓ **I must move on quickly to make my next appointment.**
✓ **I must move on to my next appointment.**
✗ *I must move onto my next appointment.*
✓ **He wandered on by himself to see the rest of the exhibition.**
✓ **He wandered on to see the rest of the exhibition.**
✗ *He wandered onto the exhibition.*
✓ **He jumped onto the sofa to watch television.**
✗ *He jumped on by himself to the sofa to watch television.*

As far as usage goes, the most common mistake that writers make is to write *in to* when *into* is required.

✓ **The rioting continued into the night.**
✗ *The rioting continued in to the night.*
✓ **There will be an inquiry into the whole matter.**
✗ *There will be an inquiry in to the whole matter.*

Also, be aware that there is some disagreement surrounding both *into* and *onto*. Not everyone accepts *into* in the sense *I am into opera music* but this prejudice can no longer be justified in everyday writing, although it might not be appropriate in formal writing. There is also some controversy over *onto*, but this is also a non-issue. The *Oxford English Dictionary* (*OED*) states that *onto* is "still not fully accepted, although it is in wide use" and should always be *on to*. It is one of the few dictionaries that refuses to sanction its use, even though *onto* dates from the early 1700s; predating the original *OED* by two centuries. It is interesting to note that despite not allowing it official status of *onto* as a word, the *OED* continues to admit that it "is, however, useful in distinguishing sense" between *onto* and *on to*. What's more, it has no problem with *into*. One wonders how long it will take before the *OED* will follow its own advice. Before *onto* enters its fourth century of use, perhaps? Don't hold your breath.

# 69

## neither...nor versus either...or
### *For neither love nor money*

✓ **He was neither seen nor heard from again.**
✗ *He was neither seen or heard from again.*
✓ **You must show neither fear nor favour.**
✗ *You must show neither fear or favour.*
✓ **In the past, neither women nor children have liked the product.**
✗ *In the past, neither women or children have liked the product.*

**Combine *neither* with *nor*, not *or*. Also, it is perfectly correct to write *neither...nor...nor* and**

There are several things to watch out for when it comes to using *neither... nor*. The most important thing to remember is to pair the word *neither* with *nor*, not *or* so that they are in agreement. *Nor* is the negative form of *or*, so the right one needs to be used in formal contexts.

✓ **This year's winner is neither controversial nor a surprise.**
✗ *This year's winner is neither controversial or a surprise.*
✓ **The whole affair is neither here nor there.**
✗ *The whole affair is neither here or there.*

It must be said that although some voices are starting to argue the case for allowing *or* to be accepted as a variant. This is fine for casual contexts, but it is far from frequent enough to be regarded as standard. Consider the following constructions:

✓ **Neither of the championship favourites France, Brazil or Portugal made it to the semi-finals.**
✓ **I would say that I am neither one or the other.**
✓ **These books are neither relevant or inspiring.**

The argument they put forward is that it is a list, not an alternative – and that it "sounds" natural to many an ear. You can expect this type of sentence to become used more frequently with time, but if you stick to *nor* only with two items then it will always be better. *Neither...or* is not incorrect but *neither...nor* is to be preferred.

Second, like *either*, care must be taken to place *neither* in the correct order of words. It must always come directly before the alternatives being listed by the writer.

> ✓ **The leadership battle is expected to be neither quick nor easy.**
> ✗ *The leadership battle is expected to <u>neither be</u> quick or easy.*
> ✓ **Unfortunately, we are going to neither Miami nor New York.**
> ✗ *Unfortunately, we are neither going to Miami nor New York.*

The word order is wrong in these two examples, not because there is a so-called "split infinitive" (which is a separate issue, see **07**) but because *neither* has jumped ahead of *be*, making the options "be quick" and "easy". This becomes ungrammatical in agreement because, when they are separated and expressed on their own, become "...is expected to be quick" and "...is expected to easy". It is *to be* that must stay together, and *neither quick nor easy* that must stay together. In the second example, *neither* needs to be directly before *Miami nor New York*; not *before going to Miami nor New York*. This incorrect word order is a common mistake, perhaps because we often say: "We are not going to Miami or New York." But when *neither* is used to express that neither one of two choices is an option, *neither* must come directly before the choices.

Be aware that there is controversy about the claim that *nor* cannot be used more than once in a sentence:

> ✓ **The winter coat was not expensive, nor too big or out of season.**
> ✗ *The winter coat was neither expensive nor too big nor out of season.*

As mentioned in the beginning of this chapter, the *neither X, Y or Z* model is becoming common, so an informal alternative would be to write it as:

> ✓ **There was neither malice, anger nor emotion in his response.**

This sentence is fine. The arguments against it relate to the view that *neither* cannot be used with more than two items – that *none* must be used instead:

    ✓ **I received phone calls from Jon, Paul and Helen, neither of whom were feeling well.**
    ✓ **I received phone calls from Jon, Paul and Helen, none of whom was feeling well.**

The truth is that both of these are legitimate sentences. There is, however, one common mistake that people make with this particular type of sentence: they write the plural *were* instead of the singular *was*, which creates a problem of agreement.

    ✗ *I received phone calls from Jon, Paul and Helen, neither of whom were feeling well.*
    ✗ *I received phone calls from Jon, Paul and Helen, none of whom were feeling well.*

Here, the examples are now incorrect because *were* is used instead of *was*. Both *neither of whom* and *none of whom* refer to Jon, Paul and Helen individually, not collectively. Therefore if must be expressed as if it were: *Jon was*, *Paul was* and *Helen was*, not *Helen were*. For *were* to be correct, the sentence should be written as *..., they were all feeling unwell* or *..., and all three were not feeling well*.

Agreement is a common area of confusion. Which of these two sentences is correct?

> Despite an extensive search, neither the children nor the father was found alive.
> Despite an extensive, neither the children nor the father were found alive.

The rules of agreement with *neither...nor* are as follows: if both items are singular (*man*, *child* etc.) then the word coming after them is also singular (*was*, *is*, *am* etc.); if both items are plural (*men*, *women*, *children* etc.) then use the plural (*were*, *are* etc.).

    ✓ **After a long search, neither the children nor the father was found alive.**
    ✓ **Neither the school authorities nor the police were ever involved.**

But watch out for Latin plurals:

    ✓ **Fungi are neither plant nor animal and are in a category of their own.**
    ✗ *Fungi is neither plant nor animal and is in a category of its own.*

Here, *fungi* is the plural of *fungus*, so the correct word is *are*, not *is*, even though both *animal* and *plant* appear in the singular.

Last, there is a lot of confusion over whether it is *neither is* or *neither are*. It depends either on your meaning, or depends on the particular singular/plural statuses of your nouns (like *fungi*).

> I have two mobile numbers on two networks but neither one <u>is</u> any good for reaching me.
> I have two children, neither of them <u>are/is</u> as successful as their Mother and I had hoped.
> Neither my wife or my two children <u>are</u> coming to the opening.

In the first example, it must be *neither is* because there are two numbers that are "no good", not both together, which would require *neither are*. In the second example, it makes no difference to highlight *children* individually or collectively, so both *neither...is* and *neither...are* can be used. In the third example, where one of the nouns is plural, the correct form is *either...are* because the plural trumps the singular when both occur together.

# 70

## imply versus infer
### *For your infer-mation*

✓ **It is vital not to infer too much from these preliminary figures.**
✗ *It is vital not to imply too much from these preliminary figures.*
✓ **The newspaper article implies infidelity.**
✗ *The newspaper article infers infidelity.*
✓ **Readers might infer that it is true.**
✗ *Readers might imply that it is true.*

**To *imply* means to "hint or suggest" something and to *infer* is to "come to or draw a certain conclusion" (deduce) or to "make a particular assumption" about something.**

These two words are often muddled and the common mistake is use *infer* ("understand") instead of *imply* ("suggest"); *what are you inferring?* should be *what are you implying?*

> What are you implying (by saying that)?
> = *What are you suggesting?* → *imply*

> What are you inferring (having read the text)?
> = *What is your conclusion?* → *infer*

An easy way to remember these two words correctly is to think: "Words imply; readers infer." There are, however, times when the meaning is ambiguous:

> The article inferred that the government policy was clear on this issue.

The danger in this example is that it is not clear who inferred the particular conclusion on government policy – the journalist or the person writing the above sentence. The writer is trying to imply that the article had a particular stance on policy, even if the reader (now writer) only inferred it. It would be better to write:

My understanding, from reading the article, is that the government's policy is quite clear on this issue.

There is a centuries' old, archaic meaning of *infer*, "indicates", but it is no longer standard. There is also some legal usage of *imply* that means, "conclude". For everyday English, however, the best advice is to follow those meanings set out at the beginning of this chapter. There is no need to muddy the waters further.

Also note that *imply/implied* is not a formal word for *say/said*, its precise meaning includes an element of unspoken suggestion or underlying meaning. If you mean, *said*, say it instead of *imply*.

# 71

## American spellings
*You can't have it both ways*

**There are many more words spelt differently in British and American English than just *honour/or* and *colour/or*. Some of these may surprise you.**

| BRITISH ENGLISH | AMERICAN ENGLISH |
|---|---|
| aeroplane | airplane |
| ageing | aging |
| aluminium | aluminum |
| analyse | analyze (see **87**) |
| archaeology | archeology |
| cancelled | canceled (see **96**) |
| centring | centering |
| colour | color |
| cosy | cozy (see **87**) |
| de luxe | deluxe |
| ensure | insure |
| enquiry | inquiry |
| fulfil | fulfill |
| Middle East | Mid East (see **52**) |
| modelling | modeling (see **96**) |
| mould | mold |
| per cent | percent (see **58**) |
| practise | practice (see **97**) |
| programme | program (see **77**) |
| round | around (see **59**) |
| rouble | rubel |
| sceptical | skeptical |
| scepticism | skepticism |
| speciality | specialty |
| skilful | skillful |
| tsar | czar |
| tyre | tire |
| vs or v | vs. |

| | |
|---|---|
| woollen | woolen |
| zed | zee |

A lot of people dismiss differences between British English and American English as "minor" and "insignificant". The more informed, meanwhile, understand that the fissures often run deeper and are more complex than is generally acknowledged.

The British never miss a chance to "trash" American English as "less developed" than in Britain, but the truth is that American English has taken many leaps forwards in making spelling more uniform. In many respects, American English is further advance when it comes to spelling reforms. At the same time these American spellings are slowly seeping into British English.

**(US ENGLISH)**
✓ **judgment, capacitive, cesarean**

**(UK ENGLISH)**
✓ **judgement/judgment, capacitative/capacitive, Caesarian/ Caesarean**

If British speakers are set against US English, then the onus is on them to learn to tell the difference between them. This way, Americanisms will not slip in unnoticed. Not every American import enters British English because it is trend (you can't blame teens and rappers for everything); a lot of change goes unnoticed because of *pore speling skillz*.

# 72

## italics
### *It is all about emphasis*

**Italics are easily overlooked in writing. There are several categories of words that need to be *italicised*. These include Latin words, Latin names, foreign words, titles of books, newspapers, compositions and names of vehicles (ships, planes and spacecraft etc.). It is also used for emphasis, but should only be done so *sparingly*.**

Italics generally differentiate certain items from the normal text. It is important to get italics right in formal, academic and published writing. There is less need to do so in day-to-day communications, such as in e-mails and texts etc., but italics should be used for web content, blogs etc. Every serious writer should familiarise themselves with how italics work.

To begin with, spell it *italics* (not *itallics*) or *italic type*. The reason for using italics correctly has more to do with style and following tradition than it is about doing something "right" or "wrong". It is not grammatically incorrect to not use them but, to a large extent, it is about meeting audience expectations. It also has the benefit of making your writing easier to read.

### LATIN WORDS

A lot of Latin words are used in English:

| | |
|---|---|
| *et al.* | *de facto* |
| *inter alia* | *in situ* |
| *prima facie* | *sic* |
| *non sequitur* | *in vitro* |
| *a priori* | *a posteriori* |
| *ab initio* | *mea culpa* |

But italics are not needed, for instance, for *"vice versa"* or *"etc."*.

## LATIN NAMES: SCIENCE AND LAW

A lot of fields of science, technology, medicine and the legal profession have Latin words that must be italicised. These include things such as biological names, bacteria, genes, fossils etc.

*salmonella endometritis*          with traces of *Bacillus subtilis*
*Listeria* is a bacterial genus    *chroococcidiopsis bacteria*
the fossil *Tiktaalik roseae*      *RP1, PTEN, zeel1* are genes
*Terra Australis Incognita*        *Terra firma*

the case, *Roe v. Wade*, 410 U.S 113          *Pv.P*[1988]2FLR307(US)
*L v HFEA & Secretary of State* [2008] 2 FLR 1999 (UK)

Note that the US system is to use *v.* with a period, while in the UK the tradition is to use *v* or *vs* without a stop.

## FOREIGN WORDS IN ENGLISH SENTENCES

The same is true of foreign words that retain foreign pronunciation, even if they are established in English. These include:

*en masse*              *cinéma vérité*
*carte blanche*         *creme de la creme*
*detente*               *lassiez-faire*
*schadenfreude*         *à la carte*
*al fresco*             *vis-a-vis*
*raison d'etre*         *de rigeur*

## TITLES OF PUBLISHED WORKS

This category includes titles of books, plays, songs and publications etc. All works should be written with italics when writing about them in text.

I remember having to read *Othello* and *Lord of the Flies* at school.
My favourite musicals are *Cats* and *Mama Mia.*
My wife bought a print of Picasso's *Les Demoiselles d'Avignon.*
I read *The Economist, The Times,* the *Guardian* and the *FT.*

Note: in some cases an alternative system is used in publishing to use single and double quotes instead.

I remember having to read 'Othello' and 'Lord of the Flies' at school.
I remember having to read "Othello" and "Lord of the Flies" at school.

## VEHICLES

Names of vehicles (ships, planes and spacecraft etc.) often get italicised. Be careful with the articles before the name itself and italicise them only if they belong to the name itself:

> *The Flying Dutchman*, the *Bounty*, *HMS Victory*, *The Enola Gay*, the *Titanic*, the *Voyager*, the *Mayflower,* the space shuttle *Discovery*

## EMPHASIS

Italics are useful to highlight *emphasis* or *stress* within a sentence.

> "Do you *really* love me?"
> Unbelievably, they had someone working *within* the organisation.

Remember that italics used for emphasis must be done sparingly. They must not be used repeatedly just "to make something stand out". An example of how this can go wrong is a press release, article or brochure where every instance of the brand or product it is trying to promote is italicised over and over. Another example would be to, say, insist that every occurrence of *they* or *we* in a text be italicised. There is no need to do this and it just looks like attention seeking.

As a final point, some writers use italics to indicate his characters' thoughts, but this writing technique is not standard practice. Yet.

## WORDS

Italic type is also used when a word is included, not for its meaning in that sentence but as an example of a separate word. You will see examples throughout this book when particular words are written about.

> Only an Australian will understand the word *chook*.
> The word *autumn* replaced the original *fall* in British English during the late Middle English period, but not in American English.

# 73

## millions, billions and trillions
### *one in a billion*

✓ **There are more than a billion Catholics in the world today.**
✗ *There are more than a milliard Catholics in the world today.*

## Write *million* for "1,000,000", *billion* for "1000 million", and *trillion* for "a million million".

Gone are the days when there was any confusion between British American English *billion* – they are now one and the same.

It is only in the past few decades that "1,000,000,000" in British English was known as a *milliard*, while in the US it was called a *billion*. The larger number, "1,000,000,000,000" was called a *billion* in British English and a *trillion* in American English.

This discrepancy did little for trans-Atlantic communications and scientific correspondence. By the 1950s, the older forms began to give way to the modern forms becoming established over a period of several decades led by the Treasury, the City and the financial press.

✓ **billion**   $= \mathbf{1{,}000{,}000{,}000 = }$ **a thousand million** $\mathbf{= 10^9}$
✗ *billion*   $=$ *formerly 1,000,000,000,000 = a million million $= 10^{12}$*
✗ *milliard*  $=$ *formerly 1,000,000 = a thousand million $= 10^9$*
✓ **trillion**  $= \mathbf{1{,}000{,}000{,}000{,}000 = }$ **a million million** $\mathbf{=10^{12}}$
✗ *trillion*  $=$ *formerly 1,000,000,000,000,000,000*
           $=$ *a million million million $=10^{18}$*

The potential for confusion across the English-speaking world was obvious. The terms are now standard in Australia, Canada, New Zealand, the UK and the US. (A minority of people still insist on the archaic forms, which are no longer necessary, practical or justifiable – even if *milliard* and *Milliarde* are still used in French and German for a 1000 million.)

If there is any doubt whatsoever, it is always best to write it out in numbers.

For larger numbers, the following applies:

✓ **quadrillion** = **1,000,000,000,000,000** = **10$^{15}$**
✗ *quadrillion* = *formerly 10$^{24}$*
✓ **quintillion** = **1,000,000,000,000,000,000** = **10$^{18}$**
✗ *quintillion* = *formerly 10$^{30}$*

The plural of *million*, *billion* and *trillion* is the same, without an -*s* on the end, although *millions*, *billions* and *trillions* is used colloquially when not using specific numbers.

✓ **The inventors stand to make millions/billions.**
✓ **The inventors stand to make several million/billion.**
✗ *The inventors stand to make several millions/billions.*
✓ **Millions of people are expected to vote.**
✓ **20 million people are expected to vote.**
✗ *20 millions people are expected to vote.*
✓ **The project is expected to cost £1.8 million.**
✗ *The project is expected to cost £1.8 millions.*

# 74

## e-mail
### *I love e-mail*

**Professional writers largely prefer *e-mail* over *email*, both in the UK and in the US.**

While the word *e-mail* (originally *electronic mail*) can legitimately be spelt *email*, it belongs to the recent e- pedigree class of words such as *e-commerce*, *e-business*, *e-learning*, *e-book* etc.

Formal writers, many publishers and media organisations on both sides of the Atlantic still prefer *e-mail*, if only for the sake of consistency. It is a good bet that it will remain for the long run, like *T-shirt* and *X-ray*. While there is no right or wrong here, the main concern should be to use it consistently.

The singular and count noun forms are the same: *an e-mail* and *lots of e-mail*; equally I sent you two *e-mails* yesterday. It has not been fashionable to write *E-mail* – with a capital E – for several decades.

From a British perspective it is perhaps unfortunate that it never became *e-post*, considering that British English uses *post* as both noun and verb, compared with *mail* in American English. (Several languages use *e-post*, including Swedish, so it wouldn't be unusual.) In British English *mail*, *mailbox* and *mailman* have not (yet) replaced *post*, *post-box* and *postman* as standard – even if it is known as Royal Mail...

I have mentioned earlier (see **10**) how amusing I find it that some people often insist on *email* simply because they say that it is "more modern" than *e-mail*, yet at the same time they insist on using *whilst* and *amongst*, which clearly do not even belong to the same era of English-language history.

# 75

## 10.30/10:30/10.30 p.m./22:00
*A timely convention*

✓ **(UK) The conference room is booked for 10.30.**
✗ *(UK) The conference room is booked for 10:30.*
✓ **(US) The conference room is booked for 10:30.**

**Be aware that time is expressed as 10.45 in British English, not 10:45, which is the format used in the US, continental Europe and Asia – and every electronic alarm clock on the global market.**

A lot of what is covered in this book is about paying attention to the "minor" details. This particular example goes unnoticed by a lot of people, but getting it right and using the right convention in British English remains important. Any writer or publication that aims to use British English (over American English) must use the correct convention.

✓ **10.30 a.m.**          ✓ **8 p.m.**
✗ *10:30 am*              ✗ *8 pm*
✓ **6 p.m.**              ✓ **6 a.m.**
✗ *6.00 p.m.*             ✗ *6a.m.*

In addition, *a.m.* and *p.m.* are best used with a space and full points. Whole hours don't need .00 after the number. Although the 24-hour clock does get used in the UK, it is not standard, nor is every Briton familiar – or comfortable – with it.

# 76

## comprise/consist/constitute/composed of
### *Comprising subtle differences*

✓ **A house usually comprises several rooms.**
✗ *Several rooms usually comprise a house.*
✗ *A house usually constitutes several rooms.*
✓ **The ovals comprise a pitch, a wicket and lots of seating.**
✗ *The ovals are comprised of a pitch, a wicket and lots of seating.*

**The difference between *comprise*, *consist*, *composed* and *constitute* is subtle but the important thing to know is how they are used differently.**

### COMPRISE

First, *comprise* means "made up of many parts combined as a whole". The common mistake to avoid is in writing *comprised of*. This word should always be used on its own, as either *comprises* or *comprising*.

✓ **Great Britain comprises England, Scotland and Wales.**
✗ *Great Britain is comprised of England, Scotland and Wales.*
✗ *Great Britain comprises of England, Scotland and Wales.*
✓ **The book, comprising 34 chapters and an introduction, makes for good reading.**
✗ *The book, comprising of 34 chapters and an introduction, makes for good reading.*

The other aspect of using *comprise* correctly is to be aware of not using it as a synonym of *constitute*. In British English a *whole* may *comprise 25 parts* but *25 parts* do not *comprise a whole*; they *constitute* a whole (see *composed* and *constitute* below). However, American English is more accepting of this construction.

✓ **The football team comprises 11 amateur players (UK).**
✗ *The 11 amateur players comprise a football team.*
✓ **The 11 amateur players comprise a football team (US).**

## CONSIST

Second, *consist* also means "a whole made up of" or more loosely "includes". There is often confusion about which word comes after it: *of*, *in*, *with*, *by* or *on*? The most common construction is *consist of*, with the meaning outlined above, followed by the rarely used *consist in*, which has the more abstract meaning "have as an essential feature".

> ✓ **The holiday package consists of return flights, hotel transfers, accommodation and meals.**
> ✗ *The secret of happiness consists in friendship and avoiding negativity and greed.*

The form *consist on* and *consist by* are archaic and should not be used. *Consist with* is also a rare expression meaning "consistent with" or "agree with".

> ✓ **The records consist with his testimony.**

## COMPOSED

Third, *composed of* means "a whole made up of several parts but not combined" and is the opposite of *comprise*. *Composed* by itself is more like a "collective".

> ✓ **Our cricket sets are composed of a bat, stumps, helmet, pads and a ball.**
> ✓ **The arts community is composed of hundreds of artists.**

## COMPOSED VERSUS COMPRISED

If only it were all this straightforward. Unfortunately, *comprise* is increasingly muscling in on *composed of*'s meaning (which also accounts for the incorrect construction *comprised of*). This has contributed to the fear of passive constructions – *composed of* can exist only in the passive (see **14**).

| | |
|---|---|
| *Passive*: | The universe <u>is composed of</u> everything that exists and everything that does not. |
| *Active*: | The universe <u>comprises</u> everything that exists and everything that does not. |

The problem of avoiding the passive sentence arises when talking about *specifics*, in relation to the *whole*:

> ✗ *The functionally illiterate comprise 18% of the UK population, according to the UN.*

While this sentences goes out of its way to put the functionally illiterate first and avoids the passive with an active *comprise*, it employs the *25 parts make a whole* construction. While some dictionaries accept this usage – which is more common in American English – it is still better to avoid it altogether. A simple solution is to replace *comprise* here with *make up*, *constitute* or *account for*.

> ✓ **Non-Western people constitute 80% of the world's population.**
> ✓ **Non-Western people make up 80% of the world's population.**
> ✗ *Non-Western people comprise 80% of the world's population.*

## CONSTITUTE

Fourth, as mentioned at the beginning of this chapter, *comprised* should not be used to mean, "is equal to". This should be reserved for *constitute*, which means, "be part of or to form a whole" or *constitutes* "be equivalent to/of" or "equal to" something, often in the legal sense. The difference between *constitute* and *constitutes* may not seem compatible but the latter is usually straightforward enough:

> ✓ **One instance does not constitute a trend.**
> ✓ **They do not constitute a threat.**
> ✓ **What constitutes "cheating"? (equivalent to/equals)**

# 77

## program versus programme
### *Get with the programme*

✓ **We plan to have a different theme for each new benefit programme.**

✗ *We plan to have a different theme for each new benefit program.*

✓ **The conference features an exciting programme of speakers and events.**

✗ *The conference features an exciting program of speakers and events.*

✓ **Computer program.**

✗ *Computer programme.*

**Write *program* for computer-related usage and the verb, and *programme* for all other types (TV, charity, course, event). The standard American English spelling is *program* in all cases.**

✓ **Would you like to head our programme?**
✓ **I saw a great programme on TV.**

Few know that *program* is the original spelling from the 1600s (in Scotland) and that *programme* arose only in the 1800s, and slowly became standard in Britain. The US spelling, *program*, has since made a return to the UK on the back of the computer industry, giving us the distinction *program* for software.

| BRITISH ENGLISH | AMERICAN ENGLISH |
|---|---|
| ✓ TV programme | ✓ TV program |
| ✓ fitness programme | ✓ fitness program |
| ✓ computer program | ✓ computer program |
| ✓ program my timer | ✓ program my computer |

The verb *program* gains a second -*m*- in *programmed*, *programmer* and *programming* in both British English and in American English, breaking with the US tradition of single consonants (see **96**).

# 78

## play down
### *cool it play*

✓ **The new manager immediately sought to play down speculation about who might be given his former role.**

✗ *The new manager immediately sought to downplay speculation about who might be given his former role.*

✓ **The Prime Minister played down any suggestion of an early election.**

✗ *The Prime Minister downplayed any suggestion of an early election.*

## Write *play down* in British English and *downplay* in American English.

*Downplay*, also known as a "fused verb", is an American sports metaphor and a synonym of *de-emphasise*. It is considered journalese, incorrect, "ugly" or all three. *Play down* is to be preferred in the UK.

This may seem like a trivial entry but there are plenty of people who dislike it, so there is still time to prevent *downplay* from becoming standard wording in British English.

# 79

## outside (of)/inside (of)

### *Are you in or out?*

✓ **You may smoke outside the house.**
✗ *You may smoke outside of the house.*
✓ **You cannot claim to be an expert outside your profession.**
✗ *You cannot claim to be an expert outside of your profession.*
✓ **These cannot be sold outside the UK.**
✗ *These cannot be sold outside of the UK.*

## Write *outside* and *inside* instead of *outside of* and *inside of*. And don't write *off of*.

In British English (or any form of English, for that matter) the extra preposition *of* is not needed after *outside* and *inside*. This includes the non-physical sense, as in *think outside the box*.

✓ **You can reach me on my mobile outside normal working hours.**
✗ *You can reach me on my mobile outside of normal working hours.*
✓ **We have a lot of clients outside the industry.**
✗ *We have a lot of clients outside of the industry.*
✓ **Let's keep this relationship outside work.**
✗ *Let's keep this relationship outside of work.*

The extra *of* is unnecessary in British English. In American English, despite being commonly heard and read, it remains common in informal usage nonetheless.

We met outside of the building.
They have developed a relationship outside of work.
You can reach me on my mobile outside of normal working hours.
Most of their clients are outside of the industry.

While its penetration into British English is still somewhat limited, it is on the rise. The influence of innovative American English and its common usage stateside may well mean, that the *outside of* construction one day becomes standard British English. That day, however, has not yet arrived, so why encourage it?

It is interesting to observe how, on the one hand, people feel the need to drop prepositions from their English in some circumstances (*on*, see you (on) Monday; *that*, this is not the news (that) I wanted to hear) while on the other hand they want to add new ones that aren't needed (*meet (with)*, *consult (with), join (with)*). In some cases, *beyond* is a better word than both *outside* and *outside of*.

✓ **Please don't go beyond the school gate.**
✗ *Please don't go outside (of) the school gate.*

Having explained all of this, there is one exception to note, namely *the inside of* and *the outside of*. Here, the *of* is required because it describes not "being inside" but the actual interior or exterior.

✓ **Engineers are working to strengthen the inside of the tunnel.**
✓ **Cracks began to appear on the outside of the fuselage.**

As you can probably tell, *inside her bag* and *on the inside of her bag* have different meanings. Here, the *of* is crucial to meaning. And while we are on the subject: *off of* is never correct, just use *off*.

✓ **I managed to get some money off Dad.**
✗ *I managed to get some money off of Dad.*

180

# 80

## one, two, three, four…10
### *Nine exceptional numbers*

✓ **It is as easy as two times two.**
✗ *It is as easy and 2 times 2.*
✓ **I am going to visit 10 countries in Europe and North Africa.**
✗ *I am going to visit ten countries in Europe and North Africa.*

## Spell out the numbers *zero to nine* and use numerals for numbers higher than that.

It is common practice to spell out all numbers between zero and nine that are written in a sentence. However, keep in mind that numbers are generally written out when they start a sentence.

This technique relates more to journalism and formal writing than elsewhere. Apply it to business writing, published writing and academic writing etc. Even if you don't necessarily fall into this category (yet) it is still worth being aware of it as a writing principle.

✓ **There were 34 people at the meeting.**
✗ *There were thirty-four people at the meeting.*
✓ **Thirty-four people came to the meeting.**
✗ *34 people came to the meeting.*

Use numerals for numbers from 10 and higher. Exceptions can be made for *a hundred*, *a thousand* and *a million*, unless they are specific (*4,500,000*). This is good for clarity, shorter sentences, consistency and easy reading.

✓ **The ship can only carry 1000 passengers.**
✗ *It feels like I have met a thousand people today.*
✓ **It is going to cost you $1 million.**
✓ **I made a million dollars last year.**

Avoid writing:

✗ *I have to fit in 2 more appointments tomorrow.*
✗ *I got quotes from 4 different builders.*

You are better off writing these out as words because they just look odd as numbers. However, use numbers when expressing units, such as *4 kg*, *8 miles*, *9 volts* etc.

The second exception is when you have a sentence that includes a list of items of large and small numbers. The principle here is to stick to numbers throughout to maintain consistency and make reading easy for readers.

✓ **Among the attendees were 11 scientists, 5 police officers, 2 teachers, 25 reporters, 3 politicians and more than 20 school children.**

✗ *Among the attendees were 11 scientists, five police officers, two teachers, 25 reporters, three politicians and more than 20 school children.*

# 81

## 30-year-old person
*How old, not how many*

✓ The artist was only an 18 year old at the time.
✗ *The artist was only an 18-year-old at the time.*
✓ He is dating a 21-year-old model.
✗ *He is dating a 21 year old model.*
✓ The 36 year old was not injured in the accident but remains in hospital.
✗ *The 36-year old was not injured in the accident but remains in hospital.*
✓ My mother gave up smoking when she was 59 years old.
✗ *My mother gave up smoking when she was 59-years-old.*

## There is a difference between something being *10 years old*, a *10-year-old boy* and a *10 year old*.

The common mistake is not including hyphens when several words fuse together to describe a thing or person.

To write *10 years old* is a simple statement of how old something is. To write *a 10-year-old boy*, the hyphens are used because all three words work in unison to describe the thing that comes after it – in this case, a boy. Omitting the hyphens here is a common error.

✓ The 89-year-old man single-handedly fought off two burglars.
✗ *The 89 year old man single-handedly fought off two burglars.*
✓ Police questioned two 10-year-old children.
✗ *Police questioned two 10 year old children.*
✓ Officers later arrested a 15 year old.
✗ *Officers later arrested a 15-year-old.*
✓ My marriage was a 10-year sham.
✗ *My marriage was a 10 year sham.*

As shown above, the three elements – *digit*, *year* and *old* – can form compounds linked by hyphens, which describe whatever noun comes after it. In the third example, nothing comes after *15 year old* so no hyphens are needed. In the fourth example, *10-year* is needed because it describes *sham* (*15 year* does not describe *old*).

> ✓ **I have a five year old and a nine year old.**
> ✓ **I have a five-year-old boy and a nine-year-old girl.**
> ✗ *I have a five-year-old and a nine-year-old.*

This is the same principle as *part time/full time* (see **54**). (For more about joined-up words, see also **44**, **52**, **53**, **54**, **63** and **90**.)

# 82

## per cent versus percentage points
### *A recipe for fudging the numbers*

**Don't confuse *per cent* with *percentage points*.**

The common mistake involving *percentage* and *percentage points* is usually to do with errors of maths, not English. *Per cent* means "by the hundred" (see **58**), *percentage* effectively means "how many parts of a hundred" and *percentage points* are each of those 100 individual points.

If interest rates go up from 10% to 12%, some people make the mistake:

> ✗ *Interest rates rose by 2%.*

They didn't. They rose by 20%, but also rose by *two percentage points* (2 from 10 is 20%, added onto 10 equals 12). If rates rose again, to 13%, it would have increased by a further 8.3% – or by one percentage point, but not by 1%. (Similarly, when a bottle of drink rises from £1 to £1.80, some people think that it has gone up by 180% instead of the correct 80%. While this is a maths problem, it also needs to be expressed correctly in English.)

The second problem, this time related to language, is the frequent use of *percentage* in general and vague terms (see also **11**).

> ✗ *A percentage of our profits will go to a UK charity.*
> ✗ *Only a percentage of staff will be made redundant.*

Any amount of money given to charity will be a *percentage*, whether it is 0.00000000001% or 99.99%. It would be more satisfactory to be specific (5%, say) or, at the least, write a *small/large percentage*, which gives some indication of the magnitude.

> ✓ **A small percentage of e-mail accounts were compromised.**
> ✗ *A percentage of e-mail accounts were compromised.*

Some people use *percentage* as a synonym of "margin", "gain" or "advantage" (*There is no percentage in it*). This remains corporate-speak.

# 83

## ranges
### *Aim for the maximum range*

✓ **We want to invite 20 to 30 people.**
✓ **We want to invite 20–30 people.**
✗ *We want to invite 20 or 30 people.*
✓ **He served in the Army between 1939 and 1947.**
✗ *He served in the army between 1939 – 1947.*
✗ *He served in the army between 1939–1947.*
✓ *He served in the army from 1939 to 1947.*
✗ *He served in the army from 1939–1947.*
✓ **I want to buy an engagement ring in the £800–£1000 price range.**
✗ *I want to buy an engagement ring in the £800 price range.*

**There are many ways in English to express range, including ...–... /from...to... / between...and... / ...or... Each system has its own quirks as well as common pitfalls to look out for.**

First, *from...to...* should be used to plot a line of continuum between two points. This creates an imaginary line, or a figurative scale and often suggests direction or movement.

> I have just travelled across Europe, from Helsinki to Lisbon.
> Go through that list again, this time from A to Z.
> She went from rags to riches.
> Our profits are expected to rise from £2 million to £4.5 million this year.

These are all correct. The common mistake, however, is to string unrelated things together in a so-called "false range".

> ✗ *I eat everything, from kangaroo steaks to shellfish.*
> ✗ *We sell everything from electronics to clothes and from stationery to home furnishings.*

There is no clear relation or scale between kangaroo steaks and shellfish, so this should be reworded. Similarly, there is no justifiable linearity between either of the items being sold. It is simply a random list that is better expressed using *including*.

> ✓ **We sell everything, including electronics, clothes, stationery and home furnishings.**

However, the *from...to...* device is well suited to logical scales, such as size (from big to small), cost (from expensive to cheap) and other pole opposites. Just make sure that, if you use an obscure range/scale, your readers will understand the connection.

> ✓ **I am interested in every field of physics, from cosmology to particle physics.**

For those who know, cosmology involves the big-picture physics of the universe and particle physics looks at the smallest elements of matter. Juxtaposing large and small works effectively in these circumstances.

> ✓ **The new menu has a selection of meals, from tapas to a four-course banquet.**
> ✓ **We sell everything from golf balls to kitchen units.**

Second, another type of range can be expressed with *or*, *to* and –. A common mistake is to use *or* instead of *to*.

> ✓ **I would like to invite 10 to 20 guests.**
> ✗ *I would like to invite 10 or 20 guests.*

Although common in speech, this remains informal. *Or* does not express range, rather a choice between two options. Inviting *10 or 20 guests* does not allow for the possibility of, say, 11 or 16 guests, which *to* does. (Obviously, if guests can only be allocated in groups of 10, then it is correct but it may not be interpreted that way.)

The *en rule* and *to* serve the same function, just check whether your writing is better served by one or the other, and apply them consistently. If you choose the en rule (–) remember that a hyphen (-) is not the same thing (see **44**) and don't use a space between it and the numbers.

> ✓ **This film is targeted at 16 to 21 year olds.**
> ✓ **This film is targeted at 16–21 year olds.**
> ✗ *This film is targeted at 16 – 21 year olds.*
> ✗ *This film is targeted at 16-21 year olds.*

Third, the *between...and...* device works in a similar way to the first two types of range in linking two imaginary points, but it does not necessarily suggest movement, nor does it include the area existing between them.

> ✓ **We have established good links between London and New York.**
> ✓ **The company directors want better co-operation between us and our suppliers.**

There might be some cases where *from...to...* works equally well, but not always. This is because it also suggests directional movement, whereas *between...and...* does not. Compare:

> We need to transfer expertise between management and staff.
> We need to transfer expertise between staff and management.
>
> We need to transfer expertise from management to staff.
> We need to transfer expertise from staff to management.

The last two examples are dependent on word order for meaning, which is not the case in the first two examples. Writers must ensure that the intended meaning is expressed correctly or risk sending out the wrong message.

Fourth, a common mistake is to combine *between...and...* with *from... to...*, resulting in a mash-up of *between...to...* or *from...and...* And rewrite to avoid using *between...–...*

> ✓ **The Second World War was fought between 1939 and 1945.**
> ✗ *The Second World War was fought between 1939 to 1945.*
> ✓ **The Second World War was fought in the years 1939–1945.**
> ✗ *The Second World War was fought between 1939–1945.*

The last example is incorrect because *between* needs *and* after it, not a *range* or an en rule, while *in the years* in itself means a range of years.

Fifth, another colloquialism is to express a single number as a *range*.

> ✗ *I can only afford to buy something in the £500 range.*
> ✗ *We would love to buy a house in the £400,000 range.*

A number on its own does not express range, although it does indicate a *level* at which something is priced.

> ✓ **I can only afford to buy something in the £500–600 range.**

✓ **Do you have anything in our price range of £100,000 to £200,000?**

✓ **We would love to buy a house in the region of £400,000.**

✓ **They want to spend around £500.**

✗ *Initial estimates put the cost in the £5 million range.*

✓ **Initial estimates put the cost at £5 million.**

Last, write *from* Monday *to* Friday and *from* June *to* September instead of using *through* (or the colloquial Americanism *thru*), which causes confusion in the UK. Some have questioned whether or not *June to September* includes the month of September, or only *June to the end of August*. For this reason, Americans use *through* (or *thru*) when the last period is also included.

In practice, however, this is not necessary. To work from *Monday to Friday* does not mean having Friday off, so avoid the Americanism *through/thru*.

✓ **(UK) The office is open from Monday to Friday.**

✗ *(UK) The office is open from Monday through Friday.*

✓ **(US) The office is open from Monday through Friday.**

# 84

## year versus annual and annum
### *Annus horribilis*

✓ **The amount of money that I spend on hotels is about £11,000 a year.**

✗ *The amount of money that I spend on hotels is about £11,000 per annum.*

✓ **We receive a yearly grant of £10,000.**

✗ *We receive an annual grant of £10,000.*

✓ **The company's board of directors review procedures yearly.**

✓ **The company's board of directors review procedures every year.**

✗ *The company's board of directors review procedures annually.*

✗ *The company's board of directors review procedures every annum.*

**Consider using *a year* instead of *per annum* and *yearly* instead of *annually*. Avoid writing *per year*.**

Many commentators on writing agree that writing *per annum* or *annually* is employed all too often as a pretentious way of expressing a year or yearly, especially when used outside business contexts. This is not a hard-and-fast rule but one that is worth thinking about.

The difference between *per annum*, *a year*, *every year* and *each year* is subtle. The Latin form provides nothing that the English form does not. So the question is: why use Latin?

A separate issue is *per year*. Many language pundits recommend not mixing *per*, a Latin preposition, with an English words if it can be avoided. Use English prepositions with English words and limit Latin prepositions to Latin words.

✓ **This is costing me £10,000 a year to run.**

✗ *This is costing me £10,000 per annum to run.*

✓ **Fuel bills are likely to rise by £250 a year on average.**

✗ *Fuel bills are likely to rise by £250 per annum on average.*

✓ **In 2010, the average salary was £25,000 a year.**

✗ *In 2010, the average salary was £25,000 per year.*

✓ **Global warming is expected to cause 500,000 deaths a year.**

✗ *Global warming is expected to cause 500,000 deaths per annum.*

There are some exceptions where *per annum* is the better choice, for example to do with wages and salary.

✓ **Account manager, Bristol, £28,000–£32,000 per annum.**

✗ *Account manager, Bristol, £28,000–£32,000 a year.*

✓ **Taxes are usually calculated per annum.**

✗ *Taxes are usually calculated per year.*

# 85

## the fact that
### *Short on the facts*

**For plain English, consider rewording *the fact that* and reduce it to *that*.**

There are several problems with the stock phrase *the fact that*. First, it is overused and rarely adds meaning to your words not already served by *that*. Second, *the fact that* does not always refer to actual *facts*. Third, if something is already a so-called fact, writing *the fact that* is redundant.

✓ **I am upset that you even suggested it.**
✗ *I am upset about the fact that you even suggested it.*
✓ **I want you to understand that pleading is not going to change my mind.**
✗ *I want you to understand the fact that pleading is not going to change my mind.*

*The fact that* is overblown and wordy. Its similarly flaky cousins are:

| | |
|---|---|
| due to the fact that | = *because* |
| in view of the fact that | |
| in spite of the fact that | |
| owing to the fact that. | |
| | |
| in spite of the fact that | = *although, because* |
| due to the fact that | |
| because of the fact that | |
| on account of the fact that | |

That so many people like to use these tired cliches is perhaps an indicator that they have less to say that it would seem. Why write five words when one will do? Your writing will become significantly more clutter free if you take this attitude.

More importantly: if something is a *fact*, one that everyone knows, ask yourself if you really need to spell it out.

✗ *The fact that the Earth is round.*
✗ *The fact that the Titanic struck an iceberg and sank.*
✗ *The fact that many people died.*
✗ *The fact that he came proves that he wanted to come.*

Another point to remember is that a lot of people like to use *the fact that* for things that aren't, in fact, a *fact* at all. Many so-called facts are dubious to say the least.

The fact is, he loves me.
You can't ignore the fact that men are better drivers than women.
I do not accept the fact that my role is redundant.
We have been talking about the fact that hospitals need to be graded.
The absence of fingerprints on the gun may be explained by the fact that the handle was reportedly covered in gaffer tape.

If you insist on calling something a "fact", check that it isn't really opinion or something based solely on your own experience. Instead of *fact* here, better alternatives include *suggestion, argument, proposal, notion, idea, statement* or *claim*. (See also *in order to*, **16**.)

# 86

## Look, an exclamation mark!
### *A mark of lost legitimacy*

**Limit your use of *exclamation marks*, restrict it to informal writing and remove them from all official, formal or business writing.**

The poor old exclamation mark is the victim of extreme prejudice by the publishing world and professional writers. The theory goes like this: anyone using the exclamation mark is either a) an unprofessional writer or b) someone trying to make the unexciting, well, exciting.

However, when used sparingly, exclamations are actually quite useful, so this view is somewhat unfair:

| | |
|---|---|
| Help! | Move! |
| Quiet! | Out! |
| Ha! | Stop! |
| | |
| I don't care! | Get out, now! |
| You can't prove it! | I love you! |
| Let's meet in town! | She doesn't want to go! |

The views on right and wrong in this instance are all subjective. (Some people also think that a mullet hairstyle is the height of fashion.) While being a perfectly legitimate punctuation mark, the truth is that the exclamation point is heavily overused. This is why it is disliked!

The need to signal an exclamation, command or order may be better suited to poetry, personal writing, personal e-mails and text messages, but it does not find favour in formal contexts, such as business writing, academia and printed publications.

# 87

## -ise versus -ize
### *National pride, and -ise matters*

**The bad news for the reader wanting to know whether to use *-ise* or *-ize* is that there is no single, "correct" answer that applies everywhere. Instead there are three: *UK -ise*; *UK -ize*; and *US -ize*. (See each section below.)**

American and Canadian writers have the luxury of safely using *-ize* without hesitation. The US is loyal to *-ize* spellings because Noah Webster favoured them when he wrote his influential spelling books and dictionaries. The *-ize* versus *-ise* problem is an issue only for writers of British English. And there is a lot of snobbery clouding the issue.

The result is that two camps exist in the UK: a minority of writers who favour the *-ize* spelling, including many academic and scientific writers, on the grounds that it is "correct" and endorsed by the *OED*; and the majority who use *-ise* spellings, which are supported among others by the BBC, British advertisers and the entire national press, including *The Times*, the *Guardian*, the *Economist*, the *FT* and the British boards of education

So who is right?

Advice on this subject is rarely clear, helpful or consistent. Dictionaries such as the *OED* usually present *-ize* as the first alternative and *-ise* spellings are presented as alternative spellings. Many people's inclination is to always go [yes, I "split" this infinitive deliberately, see **07**] with the first recommendation. However, what dictionaries don't reflect is that the *-ise* spellings are in the majority in the UK – in the case of the *OED* the house style of the Oxford University Press (OUP) is to use *-ize*.

There are not two, but three systems of *-ise/-ize* spellings: US *-ize*; British *-ise*; and British *-ize*. Before looking at each of these three spelling approaches individually, here is a brief explanation as to how the situation arose. The *-ize/-ise* mess all comes down to history. Feel free to skip the next section if you just want to know their usage.

## A HISTORY OF -ISE/-IZE

British attempts to use *-ize* are specifically motivated by the desire to follow Greek and Latin etymology while the American and Canadian *-ize* is based on standardization as a result of spelling reform in the 1800s. The British use of *-ise* is partly a preference to retain original French spellings (French is the source of most English loan words) and partly an attempt at standardisation.

English is a language that formed over six centuries from the dialects of the Germanic tribes who filled vacuum left by the departing Romans. It later blended with the Norse languages spoken by the many waves of Viking invaders and injected later still with a lot of French vocabulary used by the Normans.

The structure of English is Germanic and its spelling a hotchpotch of words from almost every language in the world. What little Latin was spoken in the early centuries was done so in matters relating to Christianity and the Bible. Following the Norman invasion in 1066, while the native population continued to speak English, French (a Latinate language) was used in the corridors of power and through the centuries thousands of new words entered the English language directly from French and others from Latin.

Among these were a number of *-ise/-ize* words. These included *baptize*, first used in English in the 1200s. By Chaucer's time, the late 1300s, the number of *-ise/-ize* words had grown and they were being used interchangeably, as evidenced by Chaucer's writing. Countless more *-ise/-ize* words were created from the 1500s onwards; this time it was new words formed from existing English words but exploiting the handy *-ise/-ize* suffix – no longer were these French or Latin originals, which by now were in the minority.

Samuel Johnson wrote his famous English dictionary in 1755, at a time when *-ise* spellings were in favour and standard across England and its colonies, although *-ize* also remained. Following American independence in 1776, the American Noah Webster wrote the successful *The American Spelling Book* in 1786 (a book that has outsold the Bible), in which he took the opportunity to introduce some of his own spelling reforms. He heavily favoured the *-ize* spelling and later enshrined them in his *American Dictionary of the English Language*, published in 1828. Webster was primarily concerned with consistency of spelling through reform rather than the etymology of words.

According to popular understanding, a group of men – dissatisfied with the shame that the Americans had a superior English dictionary – decided in 1857 that a new, definitive English dictionary, from England, was needed. A formal proposal was declared in 1858 and over the decades several volumes covering various letters were published in the run-up to the full Oxford dictionary of 1928.

This dictionary favoured -*ize* spellings following attempts to once and for all sort out the original "classic" words from Latin (-*izare*) or Greek (-*izein*). The original desire was to keep -*ize* in classical words and allowed the remaining French (-*iser*) words to stay -*ise*. This was a futile task because the sheer number of classical words that have come into English directly through French made it impossible to tell French from "true classical" words. The second, major problem with the etymological approach for -*ize* was that today the overwhelming majority of -*ise*/-*ize* words in use did not come from French, Latin or Greek anyway, instead they are words coined from others (like the recent, *winterise*). Third, across the country (and indeed the Commonwealth) a majority of writers use -*ise* spellings.

The result is a half-baked muddle in the UK and debates about which is "correct" and which is standard. Those who insist on -*ize* spellings because the original Greek spelling is -*izein* conveniently do not apply the same argument to *sceptical*, insisting that this is the "British way", even though it, too, comes from Latin and Greek thanks to *skeptikos*. The Americans, in this case following true etymology, spell it *skeptical*. It is wrong to say "-ize is correct" and therefore "-ise is incorrect". If this were true, then surely the likes of the UK boards of education, the BBC and the British media would know this, but they all use only -*ise*. It is equally wrong to label -*ize* automatically as an "Americanism" when used in British English, although it is argued that much of the appeal of -*ise* comes from being "not American".

## THREE SYSTEMS: -IZE (US), -ISE (UK), -IZE (UK)

Now for the advice part of this chapter. First, choose your "camp". Second, always remember to follow the standards of your chosen spelling category. Third, be consistent – don't mix and match. For instance, if you decide to use -*ize* spellings and write say, *generalize*, make sure that your other words follow suit. Remember your list of exceptions and don't later write: *economise*, *recognisable*, *organisation*, *compromised*, *polariser* or *analysing*. These would all be wrong. Equally, if you use -*ise* spellings and write, say, *generalise*, don't later write 'economize' and 'organization'. For US English, use *-ize* and *-yze* but be aware of a few exceptions.


## BRITISH ENGLISH: -ISE

Use the spellings *-ise*, *-isation* and *-sing* for all words, as well as *-yse*. There are only two exceptions for *-ise* spellers: *capsize* and *resize*. All words, whether they are Greek, Latin, French or brand new, are spelt *-ise*. Indeed, *-ise* is the true British standard. The only pitfall here is making sure that your spell checker doesn't keep converting your spelling into *-ize* spelling.

By using *-ise* spelling you will, of course, draw the ire of *-ize* users who will insist on so-called "correct" Greek suffixes. You may sometimes even be forced to justify your decision to stick with *-ise*. While the *-ize* users prefer to stick to their Greek roots, they must also memorise a long list of exceptions and remain fenced between two dominant and competing systems.

Some typical examples include:

| | |
|---|---|
| ✓ amortise | ✓ emphasise |
| ✓ civilise | ✓ criticise |
| ✓ energise | ✓ equalise |
| ✓ fertilise | ✓ finalise |
| ✓ itemise | ✓ jeopardise |
| ✓ maximise | ✓ memorise |
| ✓ monetise | ✓ minimise |
| ✓ neutralise | ✓ organise |
| ✓ prioritise | ✓ recognise |
| ✓ specialise | ✓ sympathise |
| ✓ theorise | ✓ terrorise |
| ✓ victimise | |

The only exceptions to keep an eye out for are:

| | |
|---|---|
| ✓ capsize | ✓ resize |

Remember that with *-ise* comes *-yse*. Write:

| | |
|---|---|
| ✓ analyse | ✓ catalyse |
| ✗ *analyze* | ✗ *catalyze* |
| ✓ dialyse | ✓ electrolyse |
| ✗ *dialyze* | ✗ *electrolyze* |

✓ **hydrolyse**  ✓ **paralyse**
✗ *hydrolyze*  ✗ *paralyze*

Regardless of whether you use *-ise* or *-ize*, watch out for *cosy*, which is always spelt this way in British English. The US spelling is always *cozy*. Non-English-speaking writers should also note that *Elizabeth* is generally spelt with a zed in English and that *Elisabeth* is generally the normally spelling in many European languages. These do not relate to the *-ise/-ize* set of spellings. The same applies to *tsar*, the preferred British spelling. The alternative spelling *tzar* is unrelated to the Greek *-izein* and the US spelling is *czar*.

## BRITISH ENGLISH: -IZE

I will declare myself an *-ise* speller here, so forgive me for using "they". British *-ize* spellers choose to do so on the premise of etymology but still use *-ise* with a raft of exceptions, supposedly because they do not derive from Latin or Greek so are therefore somehow exempt. They also spell *-yse* and not *-yze* for the same reasons, yet they choose not to follow this rule when it comes to all new coinings, such as "winter + *ize*", which is a Germanic word and also does not come from Latin or Greek.

What this reveals is that the zed camp is in fact using the *-ize* as the default suffix to all new words yet simultaneously refusing to apply it to a host of originally French words. Old and new words are not given equal treatment. Another contradiction of the etymology justification is *exorcise*, which comes from both Latin (*exorcizare*) and Greek (*exorkizein*) yet is still spelt by the zed camp with ise because it is deemed "better" that way, including in the US.

Rather than adopt the logical US approach of employing *-ize* as standard across the board, the result of using *-ize* in British English is instead a halfway house of exceptions. Both *-ize* and *-ise* get used.

Also note that *scientific writers* in the world over commonly use *-ize* spellings as standard, probably influenced in part by the pre-eminence of American dominance of science in general. Writers must still remember to adhere to the separate American and British styles.

Some typical examples include:

✓ **amortize**  ✓ **emphasize**
✓ **civilize**  ✓ **criticize**

✓ energize
✓ fertilize
✓ itemize
✓ maximize
✓ minimize
✓ organize
✓ recognize
✓ sympathize
✓ terrorize

✓ equalize
✓ finalize
✓ jeopardize
✓ memorize
✓ neutralize
✓ prioritize
✓ specialize
✓ theorize
✓ victimize

There are many exceptions that need to be remembered when choosing the British -*ize* system. Here they are:

✓ advertise
✗ *advertize*
✓ apprise
✗ *apprize*
✓ chastise
✗ *chastize*
✓ circumcise
✗ *circumcize*
✓ compromise
✗ *compromize*
✓ despise
✗ *despize*
✓ disenfranchise
✗ *disenfranchize*
✓ enfranchise
✗ *enfranchize*
✓ excise
✗ *excize*
✓ exorcise
✗ *exorcize*
✓ franchise
✗ *franchize*
✓ incise
✗ *incize*
✓ misadvise
✗ *misadvize*
✓ poise
✗ *poize*
✓ precise
✗ *precize*
✓ promise
✗ *promize*
✓ raise

✓ advise
✗ *advize*
✓ arise
✗ *arize*
✓ chemise
✗ *chemize*
✓ comprise
✗ *comprize*
✓ demise
✗ *demize*
✓ devise
✗ *devize*
✓ disguise
✗ *disguize*
✓ enterprise
✗ *enterprize*
✓ exercise
✗ *exercize*
✓ expertise
✗ *expertize*
✓ improvise
✗ *improvize*
✓ merchandise
✗ *merchandize*
✓ misprise
✗ *misprize*
✓ praise
✗ *praize*
✓ premise
✗ *premize*
✓ prise
✗ *prize (verb)*
✓ reprise

✗ *raize*
✓ **revise**
✗ *revize*
✓ **supervise**
✗ *supervize*
✓ **surprise**
✗ *surprize*
✓ **treatise**
✗ *treatize*

✗ *reprize*
✓ **rise**
✗ *rize*
✓ **surmise**
✗ *surmize*
✓ **televise**
✗ *televize*

With *-ize* in British English comes *-yse* and never *-yze*, which is used only in American English.

✓ **analyse**
✗ *analyze*
✓ **catalyse**
✗ *catalyze*
✓ **electrolyse**
✗ *electrolyze*
✓ **paralyse**
✗ *paralyze*

✓ **breathalyse**
✗ *breathalyzer*
✓ **dialyse**
✗ *dialyze*
✓ **hydrolyse**
✗ *hydrolyze*
✓ **psychoanalyse**
✗ *psychoanalyze*

## AMERICAN ENGLISH: -IZE

Some typical examples include:

✓ **amortize**
✓ **criticize**
✓ **equalize**
✓ **finalize**
✓ **maximize**
✓ **minimize**
✓ **organize**
✓ **recognize**
✓ **sympathize**
✓ **terrorize**

✓ **emphasize**
✓ **energize**
✓ **fertilize**
✓ **itemize**
✓ **memorize**
✓ **neutralize**
✓ **prioritize**
✓ **specialize**
✓ **theorize**
✓ **victimize**

The same exceptions exist in US spelling *-ize*, although it is common to see certain nonstandard spellings, such as *advertize*, *merchandize* and *televize*. Otherwise the exceptions are:

✓ **advertise**
✗ *advertize*

✓ **advise**
✗ *advize*

✓ **apprise**
✗ *apprize*
✓ **chastise**
✗ *chastize*
✓ **circumcise**
✗ *circumcize*
✓ **compromise**
✗ *compromize*
✓ **despise**
✗ *despize*
✓ **disenfranchise**
✗ *disenfranchize*
✓ **enfranchise**
✗ *enfranchize*
✓ **excise**
✗ *excize*
✓ **exorcise**
✗ *exorcize*
✓ **franchise**
✗ *franchize*
✓ **incise**
✗ *incize*
✓ **poise**
✗ *poize*
✓ **precise**
✗ *precize*
✓ **promise**
✗ *promize*
✓ **raise**
✗ *raize*
✓ **revise**
✗ *revize*
✓ **supervise**
✗ *supervize*
✓ **surprise**
✗ *surprize*

✓ **arise**
✗ *arize*
✓ **chemise**
✗ *chemize*
✓ **comprise**
✗ *comprize*
✓ **demise**
✗ *demize*
✓ **devise**
✗ *devize*
✓ **disguise**
✗ *disguize*
✓ **enterprise**
✗ *enterprize*
✓ **exercise**
✗ *exercize*
✓ **expertise**
✗ *expertize*
✓ **improvise**
✗ *improvize*
✓ **merchandise**
✗ *merchandize*
✓ **praise**
✗ *praize*
✓ **premise**
✗ *premize*
✓ **prise**
✗ *prize (verb)*
✓ **reprise**
✗ *reprize*
✓ **rise**
✗ *rize*
✓ **surmise**
✗ *surmize*
✓ **televise**
✗ *televize*

In American English, -*yze* is always spelt with a zee:

✓ **analyze**
✗ *analyse*
✓ **catalyze**
✗ *catalyse*
✓ **electrolyze**
✗ *electrolyse*

✓ **breathalyze**
✗ *breathalyse*
✓ **dialyze**
✗ *dialyse*
✓ **hydrolyze**
✗ *hydrolyse*

✓ **paralyze**
✗ *paralyse*

✓ **psychoanalyze**
✗ *psychoanalyse*

American spelling requires both *cozy* and *czar* to be spelt with zees, not *cosy* and *tsar*.

# 88

## first, second, third and last
### *At last, finally the end*

A)   First, ... / Secondly, ... / Thirdly, ... / Lastly, ...
B)   Firstly, ... / Secondly, ... / Thirdly, ... / Lastly, ...
C)   First, ... / Second, ... / Third, ... / Last, ...
D)   I will address a few points. One, ... / Two, ... / Three, ... / Four, ...

**Write *first*, *second*, *third* and *last* instead of *firstly*, *secondly*, *thirdly* and *lastly* when enumerating a string of items or points in formal writing. Avoid mixing between these two styles.**

You will no doubt see that the difference between styles A and B is that, in the former, *first* does not follow suit with the rest of the sequence. At first, it may seem that style A is out of sequence but it is actually the style that is most recommended. As far as style B is concerned, it should be avoided according to most usage guides – despite seeming logical. At the same time, the majority of language authorities see nothing wrong with style B, so do not feel under pressure to avoid it.

Confused? Having said that, a broader issue is: why use *-ly* forms in the first place?

B) Firstly, I would like to thank...
B) Firstly, I will begin by...

There certainly is some justification for doing this when a writer or speaker uses the "first-person" voice. Not everyone agrees with view but, again, there is no right or wrong in this particular matter – only convention. Who is to say that a speaker cannot choose his or her own style in these circumstances in a presentation?

In formal writing, however, the modern tendency is to lop off *-ly* and use style C.

C) First, I would like to start by...

The advantages of doing it this way are several: it is shorter, using fewer letters; lists longer than three become clumsy, avoiding the likes of "fifthly", "eleventhly" etc. once you get beyond three points. (And some question the legitimacy of using numbers as -*ly* adverbs, this is because *first*, *second*, *third* etc. are adverbs anyway.)

If you do choose style C, remember to end with *Last*, not *Lastly*. Also, avoid the alternative *And finally*.

The alternative method is to state that you want to raise several points and then list them by number:

D) There are several things to consider. One... Two... Three...

Once you have chosen between styles A, B, C or D, stay consistent.

| | |
|---|---|
| ✓ **First, Second, Third, Fourth, etc.** | **(style A)** |
| ✗ *Firstly, Second, Thirdly, Fourth, etc.* | |
| ✓ **First, Secondly, Thirdly, etc.** | **(style B)** |
| ✗ *First, Secondly, Third, etc.* | |
| ✓ **First, Second, Third, etc.** | **(style C)** |
| ✗ *Firstly, Second, Third, etc.* | |
| ✓ **One, Two, Three, etc.** | **(style D)** |
| ✗ *One, Two, Third, etc.* | |

Even if this seems insignificant, there are plenty of people who still care about the small details. If you need to impress them, make sure that you do not mix between the various forms.

✓ **First, can I say that this is an honour.**
✗ *Firstly, can I say that this is an honour.*
✓ **Last, remember to always do your best.**
✗ *Lastly, remember to always do your best.*

The final thing to think about how you end your list: do you end with *last*, *lastly*, *finally*, *my final point* or *to end*? Think about which sequence you have gone for and check whether you have followed suit. It makes no difference whether you choose *lastly/finally*, but some people avoid because of its double meaning:

Finally! He stopped talking.

# 89

## provided versus providing
### *Providing some spark*

✓ **We will be all right, provided that the staff and customers remain happy.**

✗ *We will be all right, providing that the staff and customers remain happy.*

✓ **Investing can be profitable, provided that you don't take large risks.**

✗ *Investing can be profitable, providing that you don't take large risks.*

**Use *provided that* instead of *providing that* and consider the alternatives *as long as* or *if*.**

It has long been standard in both British English and American English to write *provided that* but writers fall into the trap of using the deviant form *providing that*. Both of these are used as a synonym of *on the condition that* (older writers may also use *on condition that*).

Good writers avoid *providing that* because *provided that* is the correct form: *providing on*.

Alternatively, concise writers can opt for *if* or *as long as*, which are shorter and also sets up terms of conditions equally well.

✗ *Providing that/on I am free on Friday night, I'll be glad to join you.*
✓ **If I am free on Friday night, I'll be glad to join you.**
✓ **As long as I am free on Friday night, I'll be glad to join you.**
✓ **Provided that I am free on Friday night, I'll be glad to join you.**

There are some who do recognise *providing that* as legitimate, especially when used without *that*. Just remember that this remains informal English. Compare:

I will give you the money provided that you can assure me that it will be spent wisely.
I will give you the money, providing you can assure me that it will be spent wisely.

I will give you the money, providing that you can assure me that it will be spent wisely.

I will give you the money on (the) condition that you can assure me that it will be spent wisely.

# 90

## the tailor made suits
### *For want of a little-used mark*

✓ **I found an English-language newspaper.**
✗ *I found an English language newspaper.*
✓ **We must take a zero-tolerance approach.**
✗ *We must take a zero tolerance approach.*
✓ **Every country needs to reduce its carbon-dioxide emissions.**
✗ *Every country needs to reduce its carbon dioxide emissions.*

## Use a hyphen to form *compound adjectives* and *compound nouns* (or "fused" words).

Forget apostrophes, texting speak and split infinitives, this is an aspect of English where the UK is doing poorly in upholding good standards. The *compound hyphen* is arguably one of the most neglected areas of English usage today. Using it well will mark you out as a conscientious writer. Being aware of this particular aspect of writing – and getting it correct – separates the mice from the men (and women). It is surprising then, that not many people even know about them.

Consider these sentences:

> Can you get a photo of a high-school student?
> Can you get a photo of a high school student?
> My uncle is a criminal-law expert.
> My uncle is a criminal law expert.
> Our company just built an orange-juice factory.
> Our company just built an orange juice factory.

As you can see from these examples, the hyphen is not optional if you are talking about students at high school, experts in criminal law and factories that make orange juice. Skipping the hyphen results in students that are *high*, law experts who are *criminal* and juice factories that are *orange*. Some will argue that a hyphen is needed only when there is a risk of ambiguity, but careful writers use the hyphen correctly. Sloppy writers write *law abiding citizen*; careful writers write *law-abiding citizen*.

Sloppy writers write *only child syndrome*; careful writers write *only-child syndrome*.

In her book *Eats, Shoots & Leaves*, author Lynne Truss was right in calling the chapter on hyphenation 'The little used mark'. Few will have caught on to her play on words. The hyphen is indeed under utilised in the UK, even among professional writers; the problem appears to be less widespread in the US, and Americans are often shocked by the lack of their proper usage in the UK.

On a personal note, the saying, "If I had a pound for every ....", springs to mind when it comes to the hyphen. In my role as a sub-editor I have had countless "debates" with writers who have protested loudly when I have put in hyphens that they didn't think were needed and disagreed with me even when I explained that it was actually incorrect without one. One former colleague once objected to my insertion of a hyphen in her work by stating: "There's already a profusion of hyphens in the world."

Now, not all hyphens are the same. I am not talking about hyphens in double-barrelled words like *high-school/high school* or *ice-cream/ice cream*. I am talking about hyphens used in something called "compound adjectives". Getting these right is just as important as correctly distinguishing between *eats, shoots and leaves* and *eats shoots and leaves*.

   ✓ **I am a cross-country skier.**
   ✗ *I am a cross country skier.*

A typical example is *carbon-dioxide emissions*, which needs a hyphen. "But *carbon dioxide* doesn't have a hyphen in it," is the usual objection. This is correct, but *carbon dioxide + emissions* does need one because two words or things are being used to describe a third word – just like *part-time job*. The topic of conversation is not *carbon dioxide*, but *emissions*. In this particular case, the type of emissions is *carbon dioxide*. This is what "compound adjectives" are. Take a look at this example and decide whether or not it needs hyphens:

> The team of experts identified the need to do a small business case study.

Actually, there are many ways that this could be hyphenated, but it depends on what meaning is intended. It could be any of the following:

| | |
|---|---|
| small, business case study | = small + business + case study |
| small-business-case study | = small + business case + study |
| small-business case study | = small business + case study |

There is no hyphen in *small business* but there is in *small-business plan*. Without the hyphen these three words become *small business plan* (a business plan that is small); with it, they become *small-business plan* (a plan for small business). Consider whether these headlines need hyphens:

Small business loan plan unveiled
Tories unveil small business support scheme
How to achieve small business success
Ask the small business expert

These are all genuine headlines. And they all need work. Once you become aware of the need to hyphenate, you will see examples everywhere. These can reveal some confusing statements, such as 'Police seek black cab drivers' (cab drivers that are black), 'Government begins domestic violence campaign' (a campaign of violence started within the country) and 'Tax relief for first time buyers' (first buyers of time).

carbon dioxide + emissions → carbon-dioxide emissions
climate change + action → climate-change action
zero tolerance + approach → zero-tolerance approach
English language + newspaper → English-language newspaper

What you want to avoid is having a whole string of nouns with no association, such as:

easy cook long grain rice
a small business rate relief holiday window

You will (hopefully) agree with me that this is better expressed as *easy-cook, long-grain rice*. Having said that, no hyphen is needed for proper nouns (capitalised nouns that have unique names):

White House + staffer → White House staffer
Top 20 + album → Top 20 album
Rio Tinto + spokesperson → Rio Tinto spokesperson

Note the difference between:

public-health official
Home Office official

Now, why are we all in such a mess over the use (or non-use) of compound hyphens?

First, it is important to point out that this particular hyphen-or-no-hyphen segment is not about the separate problem of whether or not to hyphenate nouns like *high-school/well-being/set-up*. It has to do with stitching these together as modifiers of other nouns.

- ✓ **a standing-room-only event**
- ✓ **low-cost living**
- ✓ **high-profile celebrity**
- ✓ **first-half analysis**
- ✓ **a multiple-choice exam**
- ✓ **a need-to-know basis**

Many writers (and editors) either a) don't know or b) stick to the adage that they are necessary only when there is a risk of ambiguity. This approach ultimately results in warped English. There is a saying "give an inch and take a mile". Once we allow for such leniency then it ends up being abused. The truth is that these hyphens are used for a good reason. And good writers do not consider them to be "optional".

Believe me when I say that there are lots of people who take the (in my opinion, lazy) view that hyphens such as these are necessary *only* when they remove ambiguity. But taking such an approach means that they use hyphens one day but not the next. I think that compound hyphens serve an important function and like to think of unhyphenated compounds as similar to "slurls" – therapist's choice (therapistschoice.com), swiss bit .ch (swissbit.ch) and who represents (whorepresents.com) – they are too open to interpretation by the reader rather than being clearly understood.

If you – like many – never even knew that hyphens serve such a function, once you become aware of them you will begin to see that hyphens of this kind, not apostrophes, are the most widely abused punctuation mark in Britain today. Yet the apostrophe brigade, defenders of the linguistic realm, say not a word.

Elsewhere, however, hyphen usage does remain in a state of flux. When it comes to compounds, a hyphen-free world (not *hyphen free world*) causes only chaos. The best way to write clearly is to learn what they do, why they do it, how they do it – and use them.

Mastering the compound hyphen is a sure-fire way (not, *sure fire way*) to set your writing apart from every other Tom, Dick and "writer". (For more about joined-up words, see also **44**, **52**, **53**, **54**, **63** and **81**.)

# 91

## 7000, 10,000 and 1 million
### *Lining up the right numbers*

✓ **They own more than 9000 head of livestock.**
✗ *They own more than 9,000 head of livestock.*
✓ **The book is selling at a rate of 22,000 a week.**
✗ *The book is selling at a rate of 22000 a week.*

## Write 1000 to 9999 without a comma and 10,000 to 999,999 with a comma.

The thing to know about incorporating numbers into your writing is deciding what to do with *commas*: to use them or not use them? That is the question.

When including large numbers in sentences, it is not customary to use a comma in numbers *1000 to 9999*. It is customary to use one for numbers from *10,000 to 999,999*; and write *one million* instead of *1,000,000* or *1 million* – unless it is an amount of money.

This is not necessarily a hard-and-fast rule and it might seem like nit picking. Sure, a lot of people do write *9,999* instead of *9999* but plenty of people don't do so on purpose. On the next page they might well write *1275* (with no comma) without realising it. Many publishers prefer the comma-less, four-digit number simply because it is shorter and neater. Others avoid the comma because it can be confused with the European decimal comma (as in *€9,99* and *€10.700,99*).

The main reason for pointing this out is consistency. Good writers and editors try to ensure that their documents, publications and websites use only one of these two options, especially where more than one writer is contributing text. It is simply good practice to ensure uniformity throughout a document. Writing $7,650 in one paragraph and $3500 in the next comes across as poor attention to detail and appears unprofessional. At least you may be more aware of your own style after having read this chapter.

# 92

## affect versus effect
### *Special effects do not affect me*

✓ **The cold weather does not affect me.**
✗ *The cold weather does not effect me.*
✓ **I can already feel the effect of the medicine working.**
✗ *I can already feel the affect of the medicine working.*
✓ **Those nicotine patches seemed to have no effect whatsoever.**
✗ *Those nicotine patches seemed to have no affect whatsoever.*
✓ **The combined techniques were used to great effect.**
✗ *The combined techniques were used to great affect.*

**The easy way is to learn the difference between *affect* and *effect* is to think of the mnemonic: *special effects do not affect me*. This memory device does not account for every instance of *affect/effect*, but it does cover most circumstances and is an excellent starting point.**

Like *practice* and *practise*, a lot of people confuse *affect* and *effect*. Typical advice explains that *affect* is a verb and *effect* is a noun – but this advice does not make the situation clear because both words can be both verbs and nouns, and a lot of people find verbs and nouns difficult concepts (see the short grammar at the beginning of this book). Also, it is easy to be confused when dictionaries describe *affect* as "have an effect on something".

Thankfully, there is an easier way to distinguish between them. Think of them this way:

affect = this won't *affect* your no-claims bonus (verb)
effect = he is feeling the *effects* of alcohol withdrawal (noun)

This is what the "special effects do not affect me" mnemonic is based on. In the majority of cases, memorising this line will help you get them right most of the time.

Another trick is to keep in mind that turning *effect* into *affect* is usually what goes wrong, so be vigilant.

✓ **We felt the effect of the storm on our house.**
✗ *We felt the affect of the storm on our house.*
✓ **I like the effect of your brush strokes in your paintings.**
✗ *I like the affect of your brush strokes in your paintings.*
✓ **The snowstorm is likely to affect road and rail networks.**
✗ *The snowstorm is likely to effect road and rail networks.*
✓ **Smoking, drinking and not exercising will certainly affect your health.**
✗ *Smoking, drinking and not exercising will certainly effect your health.*
✓ **The virus affected five people.**
✗ *The virus effected five people.*

If you follow so far, this will be how the majority of ways in which you will use them: *affect* as a verb (*alcohol will affect your judgement*); and *effect* as a noun (*feel the effects of the sun*).

Unfortunately, there are some circumstances where the respective verb/ noun roles are reversed. Thankfully these, too, are rare. First, *effect* can be used as a verb to mean, "bring about/cause change". This is mostly restricted to formal writing, usually in the form *effect change*.

✓ **The new president wants to raise awareness and effect change through direct action.**
✓ **There is no hope of ever effecting change in my lifetime.**

Other meanings of *affect* are to "pretend" and to "act pretentiously" (*stop acting in such an affected manner*). Both of these are rare.

✓ **Americans playing Australians in movies always seem to have affected accents.**

Second, *affect* can be used in psychological terms as a noun, most often in a medical context. Doctors speak of *affect* as meaning "mood", "emotion" or "desire". Again, this meaning has restricted use and does not apply to general, everyday English.

✓ **How is the patient's affect?**
✓ **The patient seems to have flat affect.**

# 93

## criteria versus criterion
*No more than one criterion*

✓ **You have not followed these criteria.**
✗ *You have not followed this criteria.*
✓ **Intelligence is the only criterion.**
✗ *Intelligence is the only criteria.*
✓ **Your application did not meet the second criterion.**
✗ *Your application did not meet the second criteria.*

**Avoid the common mistake of using *this criteria* instead of *these criteria*; write *one criterion* not *one criteria*; use *the criteria*, not *a criteria*; and *the criteria are*, not *the criteria is*. *Criteria* is a Greek plural that often gets treated as the singular, which is actually *criterion*.**

Writers sometimes sidestep the use of *criteria* as a collective plural and might choose *criterions* as an alternative, which avoids lumping them together. This is rare in everyday English but is common in scientific language, where the need to be precise is vital. (See also **34**.)

✓ **These are stringent criteria.**
✗ *These are stringent criterion.*
✓ **these criteria**
✗ *this criteria*
✓ **the criteria**
✗ *a criteria*
✓ **one criterion**
✗ *one criteria*
✓ **The panel looked at criteria such as...**
✗ *The panel looked at criterion such as...*

# 95

## forwards versus backwards
### *Towards a backward future*

✓ **Keep moving forwards, not backwards.**
✗ *Keep moving forward, not backward.*
✓ **I look forward to our date.**
✗ *I look forwards to our date.*
✓ **This country is so backward and you, my friend, are very forward.**
✗ *This country is so backwards and you, my friend, are very forwards.*

**The word *forward* should be used only as an adjective (*forward position*, *forward thinking*) to mean, "at the fore", "ahead" or "lacking modesty". Likewise, *backward* should be used as an adjective to mean, "crude" or "underdeveloped". *Forwards* and *backwards* always denote "movement" in British English. American English does not tend to use *forwards* and *backwards*.**

*Forwards/backwards* must be used as the adverb meaning directional movement (similar to *sideways*), and in the phrase *forwards and backwards*. There is a nuanced difference between *lean forward* and *lean forwards*, but usage here is more flexible (despite calling for an adverb) unless specifics are required (*At present the robot moves only forwards and sideways*). Americans have a strong tendency to use *forward/backward* (as well as *back*) where the British prefer the adverb.

British English also prefers *heading* instead of *headed* (which is common in American English) to describe "directional motion".

✓ **(UK) Where are you all heading?**
✓ **(US) Where are you all headed?**

On a related note, American English uses the phrase *in back* and *in back of*, whereas British English uses only *behind*.

Likewise, do not confuse *forward* and *foreword*, the latter being an introduction to a book or chapter.

The same principles apply to *upwards motion* and *downwards motion*. Americans use *upward motion* and *downward motion*.

# 96

## -ll- versus -l- spelling in British English
### *Make yours a double*

✓ **We are cancelling the project.**
✗ *We are canceling the project.*
✓ **I keep dialling the wrong number.**
✗ *I keep dialing the wrong number.*

✓ **The total number of enrolled students is 190.**
✗ *The total number of enroled students is 190.*
✓ **We still own a controlling share of the company.**
✗ *We still own a controling share of the company.*

### Be careful not to let single-consonant US spellings creep into your writing.

British and American English differ significantly in the way that *-ll-* and *-l-* spellings are treated, i.e. *enrolled, dialling, controlled, patrolling* versus *enroled, dialing, controled, patroling*. This is far from a complete list, but it demonstrates that there are quite different in this matter. Unlike words that have alternative spellings, this variation is more cut and dry for each variety of English. You need to be aware of them. For British English use:

| | |
|---|---|
| ✓ **enthral** | ✓ **apal** |
| ✗ *enthrall* | ✗ *appall* |
| ✓ **skilful** | ✓ **enrol** |
| ✗ *skillful* | ✗ *enroll* |
| ✓ **instill** | ✓ **travelling** |
| ✗ *instil* | ✗ *traveling* |
| ✓ **spiralling** | ✓ **woollen** |
| ✗ *spiraling* | ✗ *woolen* |
| ✓ **signalled** | ✓ **modelling** |
| ✗ *signaled* | ✗ *modeling* |
| ✓ **dialling** | ✓ **patrolled** |
| ✗ *dialing* | ✗ *patroled* |
| ✓ **chiselled** | ✓ **cancelled** |
| ✗ *chiseled* | ✗ *canceled* |

✓ **enrolled**      ✓ **appalling**
✗ *enroled*      ✗ *appaling*

For American English, the reverse of the above is generally true.

Historically, English has a long tradition of doubling consonants with word endings such as:

*-lled/-lling* (*rival → unrivalled*)
*-tted/-tting* (*fit → fitted*),
*-ssed/-ssing* (*focussing → focusing*)
*-pped* (*whip → whipped*)

However, not all words follow this pattern (*crawl → crawled, benefit → benefited, fail → failed, feel → feeling*). Some don't change (*kill → killed, kiss → kissing, assess → assessed*).

The Americans, thanks to the success of Noah Webster's *American Spelling Book*, moved towards more streamlined single-consonant spellings (e.g. *-ling, -ted, -sed* and *-ped*) nearly two centuries ago – another example of American efforts to improve the irregularity of English.

Thus *focused* and *focusing* became standard in American English while *focussed* and *focussing* remained in British English, which has since gone over to spelling it with one s (see **57**).

What this means is that there are a large number of words (mostly *-ll-/ -l-*) that are spelt differently in British English and American English. Not all Americans agree on "single-l" spellings, but they are still plentiful.

As we all know, there has been a slow creep of American spelling feeding through into British spelling thanks to its ubiquity; a lot of which recently is through digital technologies. Books published in the UK that are written by American authors don't often get changed, which means that American spelling (*enroled, skeptical* and *analyze*; not just *color*) is often retained in texts published in the UK (see also **71**).

This familiarity with American spelling means that many people in Britain simply don't realise that *dialing, controling* and *traveled* are not being spelt in the British way.

# 97

## practice versus practise
### *Only practice makes perfect*

- ✓ best practice
- ✓ practice session
- ✓ practise medicine/law
- ✓ practise what you preach
- ✓ I am practising for the exam
- ✓ a practising Muslim

**Use *practice* as you would *advice* and *practise* as you would *advise*.**

The difference between *practice* and *practise* can be deceptively tricky if you use British English. Usage guides will tell you that it is *practice* as a noun and *practise* as a verb. Straightforward, according to some; confusing, according to many.

Most commonly, the problem is not in knowing the spelling but in distinguishing verb from noun. Again, straightforward for some but difficult for others. The common mistake is shown in this example:

- ✓ **You need more practice.**
- ✗ *You need more practise.*

You could be forgiven for thinking, well, *practice/practise* here is an "action", a verb, so it must be *practise*, the verb. This is where people often go wrong. And some of you, having read this far, may be thinking, "I will never get this". Fear not. Here is the solution:

| NOUN | VERB |
|------|------|
| advice | advise |
| practice | practise |

If you link these four words in your mind, you will never get it wrong again. (If you need help with *advice/advise*, see **22**.) The next time that you are unsure about *practice/practise*, try converting them into *advice/*

*advise.* Thankfully, *advice* and *advise* also sound different – unlike *practice/practice.* So, now we get:

✓ **You need more advice. = ✓ You need more practice**
✗ *You need more advise = ✗ You need more practise*

This simple system should solve all of your worries concerning these troublesome words. Here are some examples to guide you:

You will not improve unless you practise.
I never get time to practise.
common practice
practise the piano
practice questions
practise what you preach
out of practice
a doctor's practice
a practising physician/lawyer/architect
put it into practice

Last, any *-ing* form will use *-s-*, so:

✓ **practising**

Just be aware that American English uses a different spelling convention – with only one spelling.

✓ **(US) practice = noun**
✓ **(US) practice = verb**

**US**
You will not improve unless you practice.
I never get time to practice.
practice the piano
practice what you preach
practice makes perfect
a doctor's practice

This is helpful for American writers but muddies the water for those using British English. Even worse, US English sometimes allows *practise* as an alternative spelling for both verb and noun, which is rather unhelpful.

# 98

## try to versus try and
### *If at first you don't succeed...*

✓ **I will try to speak to him about it.**
✗ *I will try and speak to him about it.*

✓ **He will always try to win.**
✗ *He will always try and win.*
✓ **He will always try and fail.**

## Use *try to* instead of *try and* for correct English.

Although people say *try and* a lot, it remains informal English. This popular construction should instead be *try to*. The difference in meaning may appear subtle at first:

He will always try <u>to fail</u>   = *his goal is to fail*
He will always try <u>and</u> fail = *his goal is not to fail, but he usually does*

In these two examples the distinction between *try to* and *try and* is clear: the first sentence describes self-sabotage, with fail being the objective; the second describes a failed action. Another look at some more examples might make more sense:

✓ **You must try to improve your English.**
✗ *You must try and improve your English.*
✓ **Try to get here on time next week.**
✗ *Try and get here on time next week.*

While you might argue that this truly is splitting hairs, when *try* is replaced with another verb then the unsuitability of *and* becomes more apparent.

The government will attempt and build more affordable housing.
Can you swear and keep a secret?
I will promise and work my hardest.

Replace *and* here with *try* and they all make sense.

The government will try to build more affordable housing.
Can you try to keep a secret?
I will try to work my hardest.

These three examples illustrate why *try and* is wrong even though we don't always notice it. This is because we are used to hearing it in everyday spoken English. Unlike such expressions as *come and go*, *stop and search*, *go and ask* and *come and try* (which all express two separate actions).

Double infinitives can cause awkward sentences of the type:

He is going to try to speak to him tomorrow.
He is going to try and speak to him tomorrow.

It may be tempting to try and, er, *to* rewrite the sentence to avoid double *to*.

✖ *He will try to speak to him tomorrow.*
✖ *He will try and speak to him tomorrow.*

But before you do, think about whether you even need the word *try* in the first place. Your words may have more impact by being more direct.

✓ **He will speak to him tomorrow.**

# 99

## British Isles

### *making a world of difference*

**Writers need to be aware of the sensitive political and geographic differences between references to regions within the UK or *Great Britain* (Britain, GB), the *United Kingdom (UK)*, the *British Isles* as a whole, including the more general term *British*. It is a mistake to indiscriminately switch between *England* and *Britain*, for example.**

It matters greatly what part or region of the United Kingdom you mean if you don't specifically mean all of the UK. There are many important regions to be aware of, all of which have historical ties.

The brief history of the British Isles since 1066 is this:

*1066* – the Normans invade the Anglo-Saxons
*1536* – England and Wales unite by treaty
*1707* – Scotland joins this union, forming the single Kingdom of Great Britain (including the American colonies)
*1801* – the *United Kingdom* is formed when – after a personal union with England since 1541 – Ireland became part of the fold

Former names for Ireland:

*1171 – Lordship of Ireland*
*1541 – Kingdom of Ireland*
*1801 – becomes part of the United Kingdom*
*1919 – the Irish Republic*
*1921* – the south of Ireland regains independence and becomes the *Irish Free State* (*Northern Ireland* remains part of the United Kingdom)
*1937* – becomes *Eire* in Irish
*1949* – the *Republic of Ireland*

The island west of Great Britain, and part of the *British Isles*, is known simply as *Ireland*. This island has two parts:

*Republic of Ireland, the Irish Republic, Ireland*

And:

*Northern Ireland, Ulster*

The name *Eire* it is Gaelic, and although used in Ireland, it is not generally used in English elsewhere, the same way that *Copenhagen* is English for what the Danes call *København*. British journalists will also avoid referring to *Southern Ireland* because it, too, can cause offence.

As far as the various names for Britain etc, the situation looks like this:

**Great Britain** = England, Scotland and Wales
**Britain** = shorthand for Great Britain
**GB** = short for Great Britain
**The United Kingdom** = The United Kingdom of Great Britain and Northern Ireland
**UK** = shorthand for the United Kingdom
**British Isles** = geographical term that includes all of Great Britain, the Isle of Man and the Channel Islands, and all of Ireland

The term *UK* is often a better technical description than *British*. This is why there is increasing use of, for example *UK government* instead of *British government*. Similarly, we get *UK businesses* etc. *Wales, Scotland* and *Northern Ireland* have their own parliaments and ministers. England does not but holds the seat of Westminster. Each country has its own separate laws.

*British* = a general adjective that refers to individual or collective aspects of the many peoples of the United Kingdom.
*Britisher* = term used in India and the US; not liked in the UK
*Briton* = a catch-all term commonly used in the UK media
*Brit* = a colloquial form of Briton

There is no general name for the UK peoples that satisfies all parties, which is why they usually prefer to be named after their home nationality. None of the above are favoured in *Wales, Scotland* or *Northern Ireland*, where they prefer their own national identities: *Welsh, Scottish, Irish* and *English*.

*Scots* and *Scottish* replaced *Scotch* in the mid-1800s. However, remnants of *scotch* remain in the US as well as with certain foods and products, but *Scottish* is (albeit slowly) replacing it.

> *the Scots* = the people of Scotland; singular *Scot*
> *Scots/Scottish* = general term used to describe aspects of Scotland and
> the people; Scots is not used in American English
> *Scotch* = US generic term for whisky from Scotland
> *Scotsman* = older term for a Scottish person

# 100

## spell check and proof
### *Doh!*

**There is wisdom in the expression, "Never assume". Do not assume that your word processor's spell checker is set up correctly for your choice of English. In addition, be aware what language that your e-mail or online spell checker is set to.**

Try typing these seven words in your word processor now.

| | |
|---|---|
| realise | skilful |
| sceptic | archaeology |
| valour | centring |
| sulphur | |

Did they change after you typed them? If so, your spellchecker may be set to US English and programmed to make automatic corrections for you, with the unintended result of introducing mistakes to your writing.

Mistakes can sometimes creep into your work unintentionally. Your word processor, such as Word, may be set up to correct spelling mistakes as you type. If it is also set to American English then you might not even realise that small changes are being made to your spelling. While you concentrate on composing your words and tap away at the keyboard, your word processor quietly changes *realise* to *realize*, *skilfully* to *skillfully* and *sceptical* to *skeptical*. All three of these words are spelt differently in British and American English.

It is handy to have Word change a word for that you have spelt incorrectly, such as *accomodation* to *accommodation*, but not when it makes unwanted changes. This feature is bound to introduce inconsistencies and American spelling if it is not set up exactly as you want it to be.

The first and obvious thing to do is set up your spell checker correctly before your start any new document. Also make sure that the setting does not apply to an open document only – change your settings without having a document open in the programme. Select British/American English as you please and save it as a permanent setting.

Second, get into the habit of running your text through the spell checker before you proofread it. Don't just run a spell check and leave it at that, without proofing afterwards. Again, make sure that it is set to your desired form of English. Documents often start off being written by one person – such as templates – only for changes to be made by another on a different computer using different settings.

A good way to guarantee correct language when working with another person's document is to right-click on the page and choose Select All. With everything highlighted, now go and set the proofing language again. Then start the Check Spelling operation.

Remember, too, that a wrong word spelt correctly (such as *there* and *their*) will not by highlighted as wrong. In addition, keep in mind that spell checkers can be wrong and that the *British English* selection isn't always correct, unfortunately. Similarly, documents with language set to British English won't always highlight American spelling as incorrect.

Get into the habit of always proofing your text on paper whenever possible. It is easier to spot mistakes on paper than on screen and, for the reasons set out in the paragraph above, relying on a spell checker alone is a risky move.

# BIBLIOGRAPHY

In putting this book together I have, of course, consulted far and wide across usage guides both new and old, British and American. The following is a list of titles that are currently on my shelves, some of which are better than others.

**The American Language** (1979) H L Mencken, Knoph
**Better English Made Easy** (1987) Henry Thomas, Warner Books
**The Cambridge Guide to English Usage** (2006) Pam Peters, Cambridge University Press
**The Complete Plain Words** (1973) Ernest Gowers, Penguin
**Correct English** (1995) J E Metcalfe, Clarion
**Doing Grammar** (1991) Max Morenberg, Oxford University Press
**Dos, Don'ts & Maybes of English Usage** (1977) Theodore M Bernstein, Times Books
**Eats, Shoots & Leaves** (2003) Lynne Truss, Profile Books
**The Elements of Style** (2000) William Strunk and E B White, Longman
**The Elephants of Style** (2004) Bill Walsh, McGraw Hill
**Essential English for Journalists, Editors and Writers** (2000) Harold Evans, Pimlico
**The Good Word Guide** (1997) Martin H Manser, Bloomsbury
**Guide to English Usage** (1988) S Greenbaum and J Whitcut, Longman
**A History of English** (1970) Barbara Strang, Methuen & Co
**Johnson's Dictionary** (MDCCLXXIII) S Johnson, William Ball
**The King's English** (1954) H W Fowler and F G Fowler, OUP
**The Merriam-Webster Concise Handbook for Writers** (1991) Merriam-Webster
**Mind the Gaffe** (2001) R L Trusk, Penguin
**The New Fowler's Modern English Usage** (1996) R W Burchfield, Oxford University Press
**Oxford English Dictionary, Concise** (2006) Oxford University Press
**The Oxford Guide to English Usage** (2002) E Weiner and A Delahunty, Oxford University Press
**The Penguin Dictionary of English Grammar** (2000) R L Trask, Penguin
**Practical English Usage** (1993) Michael Swan, Oxford University Press
**Quick Solutions to Common Errors in English** (2004) Angela Burt, How To Books
**Style Guide** (2003) Profile Books
**Usage and Abusage** (1999) Eric Partridge, Penguin
**Verbal Hygene** (1995) Deborah Cameron, Routledge
**Writing Tools** (2006) Peter Roy Clark, Little, Brown

# INDEX